Make a Living as a Professional Self-Published Author
Laying the Foundation
The Steps You Must Take to Create a Six Figure Writing Career, Make Money, and Build your Readership

Self-Publishing Series #1

Richard G Lowe, Jr

Richard G. Lowe, Jr.

Make a Living as a Professional Self-Published Author
Laying the Foundation

The Steps You Must Take to Create a Six Figure Writing
Career, Make Money, and Build your Readership

Self-Publishing Series #1

Published by The Writing King
www.thewritingking.com

Make a Living as a Professional Self-Published Author: Laying the Foundation

Cover Artist: Wilson, ProDesign360
Editors: Christina Degano, Jilly Prather, Bonnie Dillabough
Proofreading: Rightawaywritin

Library of Congress Control Number: 2016921009

ASIN: B06XJCK6TQ

ISBN: 978-1-943517-98-5 (Hardcover)
ISBN: 978-1-943517-97-8 (Paperback)
ISBN: 978-1-943517-96-1 (eBook)

Forward

By Bonnie K.T. Dillabough

Richard has written over 57 books in several categories, but this one was most impressive to me. As with many young people over the years, I remember thinking I would someday like to write the "great American novel". I was enamored with writing. A good friend and I imagined ourselves as famous writers, living in a little flat somewhere with a typewriter and stacks of blank paper (yes, I'm really that old) tapping away as we drank herb tea and having hordes of raving fans.

This is not a book about that fantasy. This is a guide through the reality of a writing career. This isn't a book for hobbyists or dreamers. Writer's dream on paper, but in a consistent and organized way. The reality is that most books don't sell and there's a good reason for that. The reality is that although, anyone can be a published author, not everyone will be a PAID published author, making a real living from their work.

If you are serious about becoming a well-known author in your niche or genre, you need to read this book. This book is not a book on how to write. This is a book about how to get paid to write and therein lies the difference. There are a lot of books about writing out there, but very few that will give you a no-nonsense, soup-to-nuts handbook on how to make a living writing.

This is a book for doers. As I read the advance copy I was delighted to see the straight forward tone of the book and the practical advice on how write from the standpoint of someone

Forward

who makes a living writing. Richard's style is business-like without being dry or boring. I wish someone had handed me this book when I was younger. I would have been much further along in my goals to get paid to write.

Thank you, Richard. I can hardly wait to see the next 2 books in this series.

Preface

> *The golden age is before us, not behind us.* — **William Shakespeare**

Authors have never had it better. Never in the history of man has it been so easy to get your message – your book – published so that it is available for hundreds, thousands, or even millions of readers to readily purchase.

You are entering a new era for authors and writers who want to publish a book. The revolution that is occurring as we speak is far more monumental than the invention of the printing press by Johaness Gutenberg in 1436 (The Gutenberg Press n.d.), and more revolutionary than the invention of the alphabet by the Semitic people thousands of years before Christ (Crabben 2011).

This is a new age of freedom of expression, in which everyone has the right and ability to publish without going through layers of censorship and barriers to get their message to the public. No longer do you have to face hundreds of rejections from publishers before one takes pity and decides to give you a chance to publish your work.

Besides a few restrictions on extreme materials, the path is free and clear to publish any original works that you create.

You have an amazing chance to deliver your thoughts, message, and words direct to your audience.

Preface

Despite this, there are many who claim that the Golden Age of Self-Publishing is over. I've read articles by so-called gurus, saying the bubble has burst, and that it is now even more difficult to get your book noticed and to even make sales; much less make a living.

Nonsense.

There has never been a more exciting time for those who want to publish and sell their own works. In fact, the potential here has just started to become untapped, and there are phenomenal opportunities for those who are willing to put in the time and effort.

In the past, if you wanted to publish a book, you had to gain the interest of a publishing house, which usually meant you had to schmooze an agent because there usually wasn't an easy way to contact the publisher directly and be taken seriously.

Alternately, you could use your own money to print thousands of copies of your book, store them in your garage or closet, and hope to sell a few at local bookstores and pawn to your friends and family.

Those times are over. Sure, the traditional publishing world still exists, and there is value in getting books published in that manner. Unfortunately, it's just as difficult as it ever was, if not more so, to take advantage of this avenue.

In these early years of the new millennial century, you can publish your own books with your message and deliver them rapidly, or better yet, transmit them instantaneously (and directly) to your audience for purchase. You can choose to publish your book electronically, in paperback, hardcover, spiral-bound, and even in audiobook format. These options are available from various vendors free of charge or for a small fee.

This is a brave new world for those who want to become authors and the opportunities are endless, fueled by your imagination and determination.

Don't get discouraged while you are still learning how to write, publish, market, and promote your book to get it in front of your audience. Growing pains are not only natural, but necessary.

Don't worry if your book doesn't sell right away. Take it as an opportunity to review what you've done, fine-tune the message, develop promotional materials, create the perfect book cover, and so forth.

Never stop learning and continually keep updated on how to write and publish, promote and market, and about all the various options available to you.

Avoid the scams that claim that you can learn to write million-dollar bestsellers in a matter of days or even mere hours. Believe me when I tell you: every single one of them is a scam.

Steer clear of the fads or narrowly focused niche subjects and formats touted as the all-too cheap and easy answer for only a few dollars. These inevitably lead to disappointment, and don't help you build your long-term career and success.

Preface

Avoid the temptation to "jump on the bandwagon before it's too late." Take some quality time to research your market, understand your niche and passion, and build your reputation and credibility in the same way that you would for any other career.

Most of all, don't listen to others pessimistically describing how hard it is to 'make it', or that you simply haven't got what it takes. It may be a very subtle message, perhaps even striking below your consciousness, but if you put in the work, get the needed education and keep trying, you may be surprised to find you succeed.

Don't give your power away to the naysayers or doomsayers. Take their negative efforts as a good sign that you are showing true potential and passion.

Start writing today. Get your book finished. Make it as good as you can. Then publish it. The sooner you get moving, the sooner you can build yourself a career that earns you an enjoyable and decent living.

Good luck and welcome to the awesome new world of self-publishing.

Table of Contents

Table of Contents

Introduction

> *The future belongs to those who believe in the beauty of their dreams.* — ***Eleanor Roosevelt***

Yes, you can absolutely make a good living as a self-published author – in fact, with some dedication, it's completely possible to quit your day job and become a full-time, well-established, respected, moneymaking publisher of your own works.

How do I know this? Because that's exactly what I did.

My passion for writing started when I was young. At the age of seven, I found *Stranger in a Strange Land* by Robert A. Heinlein in a box of books that my grandmother had stored in our garage. Heinlein's futuristic world fascinated me with its different viewpoint about morality and the power of man.

Shortly thereafter, my mother introduced me to a public library, and from that point forward I was hopelessly in love with books and the written word. Books became my best friends, and I decided, at that wee age, that I was going to going to be an author when I grew up.

Indeed, I developed a dream to write books that would educate, entertain, and help people early on.

As I grew older, I became discouraged by well-meaning but misguided teachers, and disheartened by the difficulties of breaking into the traditional publishing world (which was the only viable publishing method that existed back in the day). I

Introduction

was then crippled by the need to earn a fast living so that I could move out from my parents' house and survive on my own, and eventually to support a family. I am sure you can very much relate to this.

Unfortunately, the need to play it safe and comfortable, at least from a fear and conditioning standpoint, got in the way of fulfilling that life-long passion and goal.

I tried to keep my dream of becoming a full-time author alive, and had high hopes of writing on my lunch breaks, in the evenings, and generally squeezing out a few minutes of writing here and there. That didn't work out so well for me. As the years went by, I became more and more frustrated, and even angry, with "working for the man", however well-paying, safe, or even pleasant it might be.

Don't get me wrong – I made good coin, a six-figure salary in fact; and the workplace was nice enough most of the time, but it did not inspire higher thoughts or ideas.

I had all by given up on the dream of creating art with words, and expected to go to my grave without making a single step in that direction.

Giving up on a lifetime desire is the point at which a person begins to die. I was lucky that I came to this understanding before it was too late.

For a creative person, representing writers universally, I became necessarily and acutely aware of how stifling my environment was, and I realized it was time to unleash my voice, which had been suppressed for over four decades by then.

And so, one day, a short two months before my 53rd birthday, after starkly realizing that up until that point, I had not made one single worthwhile step towards my ultimate desire of becoming a writer, I made the decision - it was time.

On that fateful day, after 20 years in that job, I gave notice, moved to Florida, and pursued my dream and passion with all my energy. Thus, I began my journey to finally become a full-time, professional, self-published author.

At that point, I felt as if I had come back from the edge of a precipice, and this new energy invigorated my spirit.

Luckily, I had worked hard at a well-paying job for many years, and I had enough resources to take the plunge without having to worry about day-to-day survival. Pursuing your dreams is vital to your mental and spiritual health, so make ends meet, work part-time jobs, keep your day job, make money selling on eBay, or do whatever else you need until you've achieved success. Just make sure to leave time every day to write and promote your works.

Can you believe, that this day dawned just three years before sitting down to write this book of the lifelong writing mission we share?

In the three years since, I have become a professional, self-published author. And not only have I published 56 of my own books, I've ghostwritten twelve more, ghostblogged over 100 articles, and helped dozens of businesses with their website

Introduction

copy. And the bonus is that it won't be long until I break six figures in income each year.

How I achieved this feat is an amazing story, and it is the mission of this book to share the essentials of what I've learned on the road to success.

I ambitiously took over a hundred writing courses, mostly online, read dozens of books, poured over hundreds of PDF files, examined case studies by the bucket load, and attended more webinars than I care to think about. And this no doubt helped me build my career.

However, after all of that, I failed to find the information that I needed the most: <u>How to build and maintain a career as a self-published author</u>.

I wasn't looking for a "Get rich quick" scheme or the "Write a book in 3 minutes and make a million bucks" garbage. Instead, like I said, I wanted to create a new career.

I was fortunate, and met influencers such as Ron Sukenick, Shelley Hitz, Terry Whalin, Mark O'Donnell, Ron Howard, Melissa Mabe, and Derek Doepker. Listening to these experts, along with nuggets of information gleaned from other sources, I learned what was needed to turn my dream into a money-making, long-term career.

It's a fact that the average self-published author will sell only a dozen or so copies of their book to family and friends. Don't let that discourage you – that's the way it is in any business. Making money requires effort, time and resources. Writing and publishing is only part of the job; books need to be promoted, authors need to learn their trade, and networking must be done to find people who will help.[1]

Don't despair – there are many good people who will mentor and coach you to help you gain the skills you need.

What should an author do? If you haven't written a book yet, then get started today without making any excuses. If you're working on a book, get it written, proofread, finished, and published. If you have already published one or two, promote them, and then write and publish more.

Do you want to quit your job and make a living as a self-published author?

If you do, then you need to get busy, do the work, treat it as a business, do the networking, and write, write, and write some more.

And, by the way, knock off the self-doubt and anxiety. Learn from your mistakes – you will make them – and in the process, hone your skills with education and targeted training.

You can make a living as a self-published author. The time to get started is now.

---

[1] You can find out more about how to network in my book *Network Your Business to Prosperity*.

Introduction

THREE VOLUME SET

This is the first volume in a three-volume series on how to make a living as a self-published author.

Volume 1 lays the foundations that you'll need to follow to succeed in this career. In this volume, you'll learn how to:

- Research, write and publish a book.
- Build your brand.
- Build your author platform.
- Create your author blog.
- Create your email list.
- Network with like-minded professionals.
- Find additional products and services that you can sell in your book.

By following the advice and guidance presented herein, you'll be able to launch a career as a self-published author and create the foundations for your success.

Volume 2 goes into detail about how to promote your works and get them out there in front of people so that they want to purchase not only your book, but all (or most) of your books, and possibly products and services.

Before you begin promoting and marketing your books, you must lay the foundations or you'll simply be wasting time and money. So, it's important to read, understand, and complete what's described in volume 1 before diving into and implementing the techniques in volume 2.

Volume 3 describes what to do when you have a book published which isn't selling. There's always a reason why a book doesn't sell, and in volume 3 we will go through everything from the chance that there simply isn't a market for the book, all the way to tweaking the title or cover to make it more attractive.

Together, all three volumes will give you what you need to pursue your career publishing your own books.

Self-Publishing

> *Overall, one of the things that excites me most about self-publishing is that the highest-value use of my time in promoting the books will be found in writing more of them.* — **Barry Eisler**

In the past, to become professional book author you had to find a publisher who was interested in your subject matter or your story and convince them that it was worth their while. If you couldn't do that, you could always pay what was called a vanity press to print your book, and then market it on your own.

The cost of publishing was dramatic, in that large numbers of books needed to be printed and inventoried, either by a professional publishing company or a vanity author, and then marketed and sold. In other words, many thousands of copies were required to take advantage of the economy of scale and reduce the cost to a point where a book could be afforded by your average reader.

In the past – and today in so-called traditional publishing – to be picked up by a professional publisher, you needed an agent, which is a person who knows the ins and outs of the industry. These specialists understand how to get a book published, and who is interested in what kinds of subjects. More importantly, they know the art of salesmanship, writing book proposals, and understand the politics of the book publishing industry.

A side-effect of this operating model, which lasted for many decades, was that books tended to be published only if they had commercial viability, or at least an important person's opinion. Many outstanding, and quite a few not so outstanding, stories and books never reached the public because their market was too small, too difficult to sell to, or not understood by a publisher or agent. Many great books were, and still are, rejected only because the author doesn't have a famous name or a large following of fans.

A few years ago, technology turned the publishing world on its head, and while the old traditional model still exists, it is being supplanted by new paradigms.

Computerized print shops now can print books on demand rather than produce tens of thousands of copies that need to be warehoused. Books can be printed, packaged and shipped as soon as they are ordered. This removes a significant cost barrier from book publication.

A second revolution has occurred in that books may now be published in electronic format on platforms such as the Kindle, the iBook or even the home computer. This eliminates the costs associated with printing and brings publication even closer to the author.

These two revolutionary paradigms mean that anyone who can write, draw a picture, or photograph something can easily publish their own book. In fact, it is quite possible for a single author to publish one or more books every single day if they so desire.

The freedom this brings to writers is phenomenal. Your thoughts and ideas no longer need to be approved by a third party known as a publishing company and vetted by yet another person known as an agent. If you want to create a manuscript and get it out there to the world, all you need to do is write it, publish it, and market it to your audience.

Despite these new paradigms, there is vigorous debate in the industries of writing and publishing about the advantages and disadvantages of traditional publishing versus self-publishing.

There is a certain amount of prestige with being able to say that your book has been picked up by a traditional publisher. Until recently, many libraries would not accept self-published books, although this is changing rapidly. It can also be more challenging for self-publishers to get their books stocked in brick and mortar bookstores such as Barnes & Noble, mostly because of the difficulties of finding and promoting to the right people inside those organizations.

Self-publishing is still evolving, and is quite different from what it was just a few years ago. There was a time when it was possible to publish a book on Amazon or Barnes & Noble which would sell of its own volition. Self-published authors could get away with poorly designed covers, badly written book descriptions, awful titles and substandard products.

In fact, some scam artists created applications which generated books based upon the answers to a few questions. These enabled "authors" to inundate online bookstores such as Amazon with tens of thousands of titles containing computer-generated garbage.

Other scammers created courses costing anywhere from hundreds to tens of thousands of dollars to tell you their "secrets" to getting books written, published and sold with little to no effort.

On top of that, there is a never-ending flood of courses designed to take your money to teach you how to create coloring, puzzle, comic, interview, or some other supposed shortcuts to riches.

The truth of the matter is the only people who make money from these scams are the scammers.

Today, to be a successful self-published author, not only do you need to put in the effort to learn the necessary feat of how to write (or draw or photograph), but also, publish, market, and promote your own work. You must ensure that your books are high quality and targeted toward a profitable niche or category.

In summary, write (or draw or photograph) your book and publish it yourself. You can always take another look at traditional publishing later. In fact, if you gain a following or make good sales, you might even find them seeking you out.

Ignore the scams, stay true to your own vision, and you might be surprised at your success.

Why Should You Read This Book?

Are you thinking about starting a career writing your own books? Are you looking at self-publishing as opposed to traditional publishing? Are you working on your first book and don't know how to move forward, or have you written several books that never seem to sell?

The world of self-publishing can appear complicated and overwhelming. There are many moving parts and it is important to understand what is useful and what can be ignored.

Also, there are an extraordinarily large number of voices claiming – no, screaming – that they know exactly how you can make thousands of dollars a day or six-figure incomes or become a millionaire or some other mindless platitude. These glittery, tempting offers add even more confusion to the picture and usually don't produce any real or lasting results – if they produce anything at all.

This book guides you through what you need to do to be a self-published author and make an income that can support you and your family. Of course, there are no promises, as the results depend upon your skills, abilities, schooling (both past and present), and the amount of effort that you're willing to put in, combined with just a little bit of luck.

If you're looking for a practical map that helps you make sense of all the confusion, then read this book. On the other hand, if you are searching for a quick and easy way to make a buck, you'll be disappointed by what I've written.

In summary, what I'm going to tell you is how to build a long-term career as a self-published author, publisher and promoter. It's not an easy path, but then neither is becoming a doctor, physical therapist, or musician. A fulfilling career requires work, training, time, and a willingness to do what's necessary.

There are many, many ways to make a living as an author and a writer. This book explains the steps that I have taken to accomplish this goal. There are other methods which may or may not work; however, what I describe in the following pages has the advantage in that it has been well-tested by the Writing King.

Good luck and I hope you enjoy the ride.

EXERCISES

The purpose of this book is to help you get started and succeed as a self-published author. This requires more than reading a book – you must get out in the world, both on and off-line, and walk the walk, so to speak.

The exercises following some of the sections and chapters are designed to get you to do the actions needed to be a professional writer.

In other words, if you do these exercises honestly and completely, by the time you finish this book you'll be well on your way.

To begin, get yourself a notebook, anything will do although one of those loose-leaf three-ring binders would be perfect, and some pens or pencils. Or use an online app to track your progress. You'll need those to complete the exercises.

P.S. (NOTES ABOUT THE CONTENT)

There are instances in which this book directly references pages on the web for more information. Sometimes the tutorials and online help files provided by various companies describe how to use their product or service better than I could in this volume. There is no need to duplicate information that already exists elsewhere.

Long links (URLs) are difficult to type, so I've used two link shorteners to help: mybooks.space and smooth.li. The purpose is to make it easier to type the URL into your web browser.

I have not included screenshots within this book as most companies, such as Amazon, frown on their inclusion. In addition, in many cases using them will violate their terms and condition. Besides, applications change regularly and screenshots will quickly become obsolete.

I hope you enjoy what I've written and find it to be of some value. If you would like to send me a note about this book, feel free to write me at rich@thewritingking.com. If you enjoy the book, please write a positive review on Amazon.

Chapter 1
The Basics

> *Technology now allows people to connect anytime, anywhere, to anyone in the world, from almost any device. This is dramatically changing the way people work, facilitating 24/7 collaboration with colleagues who are dispersed across time zones, countries, and continents.* — **Michael Dell**

Before diving into how to create a career as a self-published author, I want to spend a few minutes going over something I call "the writing life."

By "the writing life", I'm specifically referring to the lifestyle as a self-published author who is making a prosperous living in that line of work. This is different than the lives of the freelance writer or the copywriter who answer to clients. Instead, in the 'self-published writing life', you answer to your readers.

In my mind, this is one of the things that is attractive about being a self-published author – not answering to a client, a boss, or a manager. The people I answer to are the direct purchasers of my products; my books and related materials.

I worked in a "9-to-5" job (although for my entire career it was closer to 24/7) for my entire adult life up until I retired a few years ago. The mythology associated with working a normal job is that you get a steady paycheck, fair reviews from your manager, benefits, and have some stability. There is also a widely-held belief that under normal conditions, you can't be fired or terminated without good cause.

Chapter 1
The Basics

Naturally, in return, you are expected to produce whatever it is you have been hired to create in a reasonable timeframe, with good quality.

The reality is quite different. In virtually every state in the United States, an employee can be fired for any reason (excluding those which fall under protected categories) at any time, to become instantly jobless without notice. Companies do this all the time – larger corporations can lay off tens of thousands of people if their industry changes or when their managers make bad decisions.

In general, working a "regular" job does give you a steady paycheck, a certain degree of stability, and those all-important benefits – or at least an illusion of safety.

However, you lose a lot of control over your own life by working at a job. You must arrive at work at a prescribed time, take more regimented breaks, receive reviews from someone who doesn't even understand what you're doing for the most part, and more or less do what you're told to.

That's the reality of working a "9-to-5 job". It's not always negative – in fact it can be quite pleasant. On the bright side, you get to work with a team of people who can stimulate your sensibilities and expand your horizons, not to mention provide a social milieu of support, and even entertainment.

The writing life is quite different. I work from home, sometimes spending half the day in my pajamas, only dressing up when I need to go out to a networking meeting, give a speech at Toastmasters, watch a movie at the local theater, or go on a date. My normal attire, if I'm not in PJs, is jeans and Hawaiian shirts, and in the day, you can find me sitting under a large umbrella next to the pool, happily typing away on my laptop.

https://www.toastmasters.org/

For those who have families, the writing life means spending more time at home with the kids and the spouse or significant other. That's one of the huge advantages of this lifestyle, because a "normal" job eats up the most important hours of the day.

For stay-at-home parents or people with disabilities, the writing life can be an excellent way to make a living without having to struggle to find a reliable and affordable daycare, or a way to get to work every day.

Once a steady income has been established, the freedom can be incredible. I spend much of my day writing, but the Muses (another word for creative impulses) visit at different times, making it difficult to stick to the kind of schedule that is necessary in a normal job.

Of course, there are downsides, even to the best of things. If you are not careful to establish multiple streams of income, you can find yourself scrambling for money if something stops selling due to changes in the economy or public taste.

That's a subject we're only going to touch upon lightly in this book: establishing more than one income stream. In my case, I receive money from my self-published books, freelance work such as ghostwriting and blogging, and drop shipping on eBay. I know that sounds like a lot of work, but any one of those arenas could cease and it wouldn't dramatically affect my lifestyle.

A strategy that works for books is to write and publish as many as you can because it is simply natural that you'll have a varying degree of success. Your income will not depend on one or two books; instead it will be drawn from all of them.

ANYONE CAN PUBLISH A BOOK

> *I wrote a book. It sucked. I wrote nine more books. They sucked, too. Meanwhile, I read every single thing I could find on publishing and writing, went to conferences, joined professional organizations, hooked up with fellow writers in critique groups, and didn't give up. Then I wrote one more book.* — **Beth Revis**

These days anyone can publish a book, long or short, about virtually any subject, for little to no cost, other than your precious time. This environment has created the *illusion* that writing and publishing is trivial and the field is wide-open for making easy money without effort.

There are hordes of unscrupulous individuals and businesses who will claim to know the secret formula, say they have cracked the code, learned how to cast the spells to take advantage of the "easy money" of self-publishing[2]. They wildly

---

[2] While it might seem reiterative to repeat the warnings about scams several times in this book, it's important to understand that you will run into them often in your writing career. There are many dishonest people who want to deprive you of your hard-earned money without giving you any real benefit. It's vital that you keep your eyes open and do not waste your money, time and energy on get-rich-quick

proclaim that you can create books in less than an hour and have three or four of them published and making money by the end of the day. Naturally, to learn their secrets you must pay a small fee of anywhere from $9.95 all the way up to $50,000 (payable in 3 easy payments), or more.

Unfortunately, despite the advice of these so-called experts, making a living as a self-published author is not an easy career. The learning curves are steep, and there are many specialties which you will either need to understand, or hire someone to execute for you.

Making a living, which I define as earning at least $60,000 a year, as a self-published author is not a game for the weak of heart. Then again, doing anything of value such as becoming a doctor, fireman, an astronaut, or composer requires years of effort, specialized training, and being willing to take the time and spend the money to learn how to do it.

Anyone can publish a book. A professional takes the time to write a quality work that delivers a clear message, is free of grammar and spelling errors, and is promoted correctly to the right audience. When you take on the role of a professional author, you have a responsibility to yourself and your readers.

By being a professional, and acting like one, you'll find that you are treated with respect, your books will sell better, and you will raise above the rest of the pack.

---

schemes, regurgitated courses, overpriced products, and even illegal pyramid schemes.

Chapter 1
The Basics

BE A PROFESSIONAL

There was a moment when I changed from an amateur to a professional. I assumed the burden of a profession, which is to write even when you don't want to, don't much like what you're writing, and aren't writing particularly well. — **Agatha Christie, An Autobiography**

Writing is a profession, and if you want to establish a career, you should be and act like a professional. This means that you operate in such a way that you respect yourself, and others, in turn, respect you.

Some of the characteristics of a professional are listed below:

- You've made a commitment to succeed.
- You strive to develop and improve your skills.
- You are competent.
- You are honest and have integrity.
- You are accountable for your actions.
- You remain in control.
- You maintain a good image.

Let's go over each one of these in a bit more detail as they apply to being a self-published author.

Commitment and Discipline – If you want to be successful as a self-published author, you must make a commitment to yourself that you will do whatever it takes, within the bounds of ethics, to succeed. This means you'll put in the time and effort to do what needs to be done.

For professional writers and self-publishers, this means writing, promoting, marketing, and publishing even when you want to do something else or are "not in the mood."

Improve your skills – Professionals constantly learn about their vocation. You should be attending courses, reading books, finding references, learning grammar and spelling, attending critique meetings, and doing everything else you can to make yourself a better writer, publisher, marketer, and promoter.

Competent – You get the job done, you're reliable, and if you make a promise you keep it. As a self-published author, many of your commitments will be to yourself as you set goals and targets, define priorities, and decide what needs to be done. For your own self-esteem, achieve what you set out to do. If you fail, learn from the failure and move forward.

Another part of competency is to know how to use your tools to your best advantage. In the field of writing, you might be working on a computer using a word processor. Understand these and your other tools, taking related courses as needed, to become proficient in their use.

Honesty and integrity – You keep your word and you can be trusted. The promises that you make will be to yourself and are the easiest ones to let slide because no one else will know. It's important for your own self-respect to keep your word and know that you can trust yourself; it's equally important for your credibility to keep your promises, including deadlines, to others.

Chapter 1
The Basics

Accountable – If you make a mistake, admit it, learn from it, and move on. It's the same with success – when you succeed, pat yourself on the back, learn why you succeeded, and then move on to the next thing.

Remain in control – Whatever happens, keep your emotions in check, and don't doubt yourself. You are going to make mistakes; that's a part of life; don't dwell on them. When things get frantic, as when you're publishing your book, or doing lots of promotions, keep your cool and follow your plans and checklists.

Image – this can be a tough one for self-published authors, because they work from home. Sure, you can work in your pajamas, get out of bed when you want, maybe drink a little bit too much. After all, there's no boss to yell at you.

Well, that's not quite true. When you work from home, you are your own boss and your own employee. Look at yourself from both sides and make two report cards for yourself. As a boss, are you an inspirational leader, a great role model, and an expert in your field? As an employee, are you reliable and productive, agreeable and respectful?

Maintain a professional demeanor. If working in PJs makes it more comfortable and supports productivity then, by all means, do so, however it is important to feel your cred, so do what it takes to feel professional. And when you go out in public, or have a virtual meeting on Skype, present a polished image.

By being a professional, you will feel better about yourself and it will be easier for you to meet your objective of making a good income as self-published author.

GRAMMAR, SPELLING AND STYLE

> *It's hard to take someone seriously when they leave you a note saying, 'Your ugly.' My ugly what? The idiot didn't even know the difference between your and you're.* — **Cara Lynn Shultz, Spellcaster**

As a writer, your primary tool is the written word in your language of choice. Because of that, your most important tools are a style manual, a dictionary, a thesaurus, and a grammar handbook.

For English, I recommend that you purchase *The Chicago Manual of Style, 16th edition*, in hardcover format. This book will be invaluable to you as you write and have questions about grammar, writing styles, citations, and anything else related to writing.

Find a good dictionary; not an overly simple one, or a complex, unabridged version. Small dictionaries don't have enough meanings, and therefore are confusing and limited. Large, unabridged dictionaries have too many meanings which can also lead to confusion and overwhelm you.

Finding a good dictionary requires a trip to a bookstore. Grab a few dictionaries, and bring them over to a table in the store, and thumb through them. Look up a few words in each one and see if it does what you need. Purchase the one with

Chapter 1
The Basics

understandable definitions, good derivations, and whatever else you think you need to help define words. You can also use online dictionaries as well, but be sure to find one that has good definitions, idioms, and derivations.

Another book that can come in handy is a thesaurus. As you write, you may find you are using the same word repeatedly throughout your text. To make your writing more interesting, use a thesaurus to find other words that fit. You will also expand your vocabulary, which will make you a better writer.

Finally, a small grammar book is useful, but not essential. I use a book called *The Only Grammar Book You'll Ever Need*, by Susan Thurman. This contains most of the grammatical rules that you'll need and it's much simpler than the style manual.

It's important that a writer spell correctly and use proper grammar. Nothing makes you look more unprofessional than misspelled words, improper grammar, and poor style. However, this is tempered by the fact that there will always be a mistake or two in your books. Don't beat yourself up if someone finds a grammar or spelling error (or two or three) in a book you've published. The beauty of self-publishing is that you can make corrections and republish at any time.

Exercise: Take a trip to your local library to examine dictionaries, grammar books, and style manuals. Borrow a few (if possible) so you can test them all out for a week or two. Once you've found the books that work for you, buy copies for yourself.

THE HURDLES TO BE OVERCOME

Sometimes the hurdles aren't really hurdles at all. They're welcome challenges, tests. — **Paul Walker**

There are three major hurdles to overcome in order to succeed. In fact, you will need to scale these hurdles repeatedly if you want to make a long-term living in this field. Don't despair, however, as it will become easier each time you go through the process, until eventually you'll forget that you ever thought that it was difficult.

First, you need to research, then write your book and get it ready for publication. Second, you need to publish that book to one or more platforms such as Amazon, iBook, Nook and so forth. Third, you must build an audience of people who want to buy not just one book, but many books from you. In order to sell to them you'll practice public relations, marketing, and promotion.

However, since the cost of self-publishing is now free in most instances, the marketplace is being inundated with thousands of new books published every single day. This is one of the reasons why it can be difficult for an author to sell their works.

While it is no doubt challenging to write a book, and there is a large learning curve associated with publishing, the real problem faced by most authors, both self-published and traditional, is getting their book in front of their public. In other words, reaching people interested in their subject enough to purchase and read their works.

Chapter 1
The Basics

When you self-publish a book, you're faced with a dilemma similar to trying to get people to notice a single snowflake during a raging blizzard.

The quality of your book or the importance of your subject is irrelevant if no one can find it. To sell on Amazon, for example, a book needs to be on the first page or two of search results for any category or search phrase. Most people will not look beyond the first several pages to find what they want.

Nonetheless, don't despair. There is hope for self-published authors.

I've said this before, and I'll say it again. You _can_ make a good living by writing and selling your own books. It is challenging, but the challenge is the same as with any small business attempting to sell its products or services. Products, in this instance books, must be conceptualized, written, edited, proofread, published, promoted, marketed, revised, and so forth.

The key factor is to educate yourself and refine your process in terms of priorities and focus.

You can master all the skills needed to publish your own books. Take each step one at a time, move forward, and don't worry too much about failure. In fact, you should come to embrace failures because of the lessons that you'll learn from each one.

- Research your niche or category to find a topic, fiction or nonfiction, that is likely to be profitable.
- Write, edit, and proofread your book.

- Build the audience before and after your book has been published.
- Publish your book using Amazon or one of the other publishing services.
- Market and promote yourself and your books to the correct audience.

Once you've mastered each of these steps, you'll be on your way to becoming a successful, self-published author.

THERE IS ONLY SO MUCH TIME IN A DAY

The bad news is time flies. The good news is you're the pilot. — **Michael Altshuler**

If you try to do everything that's possible, you will quickly be overwhelmed and won't get much done at all. As a self-published author, you wear many hats:

- running a business
- accounting
- writing your books
- editing
- proofreading
- producing book covers
- creating a website or blog
- writing promotional copy
- understanding and handling any legal issues

We'll go through all the steps necessary to write, publish and promote a book in the rest of this volume.

Chapter 1
The Basics

But let me tell you, there are a lot of steps, a lot of options, and many things that need to get done. It can be very overwhelming, especially when something doesn't work as expected, or takes far longer than anticipated.

The key is to figure out what you're good at, and what you like to do. For example, many authors enjoy writing but don't know how to use a graphics program and haven't been trained in artistic design, which are skills required for creating a decent book cover.

In this case, don't spend days trying to figure out that cool graphics editing application. It's a better use of your time to find someone who can create your book cover for you.

You can hire a freelancer to perform that task and save yourself the time and frustration. There are some excellent book cover artists on websites such as Fiverr.com who will be happy to do good quality work for you for as little as $5.

Another option is to trade services with someone else who's good at something you need but would like some writing done. For example, I've written blog articles in exchange for book covers, saving myself the hassle, and helping another author out as well.

As time goes by, build yourself a network of people you can delegate specialized tasks to, in order free up your time and ultimately focus on what you do best.

For example:

- I use a freelance artist on Fiverr.com to create covers for my eBooks, paperbacks, hardcovers, and audiobooks.
- For my coloring books, I've hired half a dozen artists at widely varying costs to draw the coloring pages.
- I've also hired people on Fiverr.com to do my proofreading, editing, promotion, and even the copy for my Amazon book descriptions.
- A graphics artist created my logo and the graphics for my website, and an SEO expert worked to get Google and Bing to send traffic my way.

We'll go into the techniques you can use to build a writing network later in this book, as it's critical to your success as a self-published author. The simple fact of the matter is that if you want to make a living in this field, or in any field really, you need to work with many experts for mutual support, which can thus improve your ability to get things done efficiently and professionally.

Chapter 1
The Basics

> *Decide what you want, decide what you are willing to exchange for it. Establish your priorities and go to work.* — **H. L. Hunt**

As we discussed in the last section, you can only get so much done each day. As you proceed through the process of building and maintaining your writing career, you'll find yourself with a plethora of tasks that need to be completed – some small and others much larger.

Devote a portion of your production time every day to writing and publishing. This is because one of the highest priorities of a self-published author is to write a large quantity of books that you can publish and put up for sale. To keep that quantity rising, you need to be writing and publishing books consistently and constantly.

To manage all the tasks and to give the chaos some sort of order, create a prioritized to-do list. This will help prevent you from being overwhelmed by the immense number of tasks that pop up all the time, each demanding your immediate attention and action.

I recommend allocating at least 50% of each workday to actively writing and publishing your books. Split the other 50% up based upon your other priorities. By doing this you will continue to write steadily, but still manage to get other important tasks completed.

Writing goes at the top of the list, and anything that directly produces income gets placed next. Since I'm also a freelance writer, any paid projects get done only after working on my own books.

Promotional tasks need to come next, since they are required to make income over the short and long-term. Without promotion, sales don't occur.

Other tasks get prioritized depending upon their importance, which may be based on a variety of factors.

Don't be alarmed at the number of low-priority tasks that accumulate on your list. This is good management because when those tasks become more important, they will naturally bubble up to the top.

After a year of writing, publishing, and promoting 56 different books, you can probably guess that I accumulated a huge amount of these lower-priority items.

To prevent them from getting lost, I created a notebook, one of those three ring binders with dividers to organize things. In that notebook, I keep track of each of the tasks for each of the different areas of my business.

There are several online applications or programs which will help you create prioritized to-do lists, and multiple generations of tasks with deadlines and prompts. One hint here is you should always set the alarms or notifications.

This keeps me from losing or forgetting about the lower-priority items. I intend to get to them someday, but they are not important to do right now.

Chapter 1
The Basics

For example, I published a dozen coloring books and then received advice that it would be better if they had a page at the front titled "this book belongs to." Creating twelve pages (one for each book) is not a lot of work, but inserting a page into each and republishing them could take a lot of time – perhaps a whole day, for all twelve. Since this task is more of a "nice to have," it was recorded in the 3-ring binder and put aside for the time being.

Once I've accumulated several related tasks, I may block out some time to get through them all. For example, my list for coloring books included

- creating "this belongs to" page
- adding an advertisement to the back for all of them
- updating the copyright notice
- including a short, half page story of why the book was written
- republishing the books with the new material

Since there were now several tasks that could be worked at the same time, I blocked out several hours and powered through all of them in a single sitting. This used my time far more effectively than trying to do each one individually.

Every day, I make it a point to reach down into my low priority task book and complete at least one of them. Sometimes they only take a few minutes, and sometimes they require as much as an hour. It gives me an added feeling of accomplishment to get some of these "nice to have" items completed regularly.

Exercise - Get a piece of paper and write down, off the top of your head, 10 things that you need to do to get your book written, published and promoted. Examine your list and put them in priority order, numbering from one, the highest priority, to 10, the lowest priority.

SET GOALS

> *Your goals are the road maps that guide you and show you what is possible for your life.* — **Les Brown**

It's important, as you evolve through your writing career, to set goals so you have a good idea of where you're going. Once you set a goal, you can define the tasks (and sub-tasks) that you need to do to achieve that objective. Additionally, goals allow you to differentiate tasks based upon whether they help you reach the target or not.

The best goals are SMART (Drucker 2006), which stands for Specific, Measurable, Achievable, Realistic and Time bound.

Specific - Goals need to be specific and not general. For example, instead of saying, "complete writing a book by the end of the month," define your goal as, "Complete the first draft of the book *How to Peel Potatoes* by the first of January."

Measurable - They should also be something that you can see in the physical universe or measure; in other words, they need to be concrete and not abstract. "Complete the writing of a specific book within a month" is a great goal. "Becoming more knowledgeable about computer security," is not a good goal because it can't be measured.

Chapter 1
The Basics

Achievable - You need to make sure that you can achieve them, considering all the other things that you need to do during that time. Remember to factor in life and living; for example, if you need to spend two hours a day bringing the kids to and from school, and another two hours cooking, make sure your target date takes that into account.

Realistic - Set realistic goals that you can and do accomplish. If you consistently set targets that you never meet, you'll become frustrated.

Time Bound - Goals should always include a completion date because otherwise they tend to float into the future and may never get done.

For example, if your goal is to get a book called *How to Peel Potatoes* published by the end of the month, then you can define the tasks that you need to complete to reach that goal, and set dates on those tasks.

Your tasks might include writing the book, getting it proofread, having somebody else read it, creating the cover, publishing it, and doing the appropriate promotional steps.

Exercise - Set a SMART goal for how many words you are going to write for the day, then go ahead and write that many words. Did you set your goal too high? Too low? Or was it just right? Did distractions get in your way? Make a note of all the things that prevented you from meeting your goal. What can you do about them?

THE DISTRACTIONS

One way to boost our will power and focus is to manage our distractions instead of letting them manage us. —**Daniel Goleman**

Throughout your day, you'll find there are many distractions that chip away at your time and reduce your productivity. It's vital to your success as a self-employed person to identify and eliminate these distractions as much as you can. Otherwise, you'll get to the end of each day without much accomplished, wondering where the hours went.

Writing and answering emails that have no business purpose, chatting on the phone, talking with people who happen to stop by, and social media are some of the things that will drain your time. These interruptions taken individually may be small and harmless but when taken together as a whole can dramatically affect your productivity throughout the day.

Social media such as Facebook will totally eat away at your precious time and attention to annihilate the best laid plans to complete your tasks. Many people install social media applications on all their devices, and allow all notifications, so that these devices will be continually pinging, beeping, or flashing.

The Facebook wall can be especially distracting to a writer, especially when facing a writer's block. The funny thing is virtually all postings are utterly unimportant at the end of the day.

To control the wall, you can install a Chrome extension called Kill News Feed. This essentially deletes the wall from

Chapter 1
The Basics

Facebook. You still have access to groups, messages, and everything else, but the main wall becomes a blank space.

Click the following link to download this Chrome extension.

http://smooth.li/kill-news-feed

Regardless of whether you install this extension, social media such as Facebook, Google Plus, LinkedIn, Twitter, and all the rest will beckon to you all day long.

Then there is the distraction of solitude. I find that sitting in a chair most of the day, staring at a computer screen tends to make me crave contact with people, even though I tend to be a bit of a loner and introverted. Thus, when the opportunity to chat or talk with someone arises, I welcome it and totally chillax.

My recommendation is to schedule social media and social interaction at specific times of the day, and limit those activities to a set amount of time. For example, my habit is to address social media for half an hour each morning as soon as I get up, and a half hour each evening just before going to bed.

Exercise: Look over your space. Do you have a special place, a sanctuary of sorts, where you can write in peace? Look for a room with a good desk, chair and without a television, video games, or other distractions. Set this space up, as best you can, as your office and make sure you have everything you need close to hand.

PROFESSION OR HOBBY?

I don't have time for hobbies. At the end of the day, I treat my job as a hobby. It's something I love doing. — **David Beckham**

To make a steady income writing, you must treat it like you would any other profession. In other words, you need to put in the time and effort to make it happen because books don't normally just sell themselves.

You must treat your writing career seriously. This means, treat it as a business, with everything this implies. For example, you'll need to be concerned with paying taxes, keeping your accounting, and even small and tedious things such as ensuring you have a local business license to legally work out of your home.

Hobbies, even if they make a little money, don't require that much effort. Making a living requires that you ensure that the basics are being handled on a day-to-day basis.

WORD COUNT GOALS

Every secret of a writer's soul, every experience of his life, every quality of his mind, is written large in his works. — **Virginia Woolf**

We'll go into much more detail about this later in this book, but it should be obvious that writers need to write.

The method you use to do so is not relevant – the important thing is that you write, and you write as much as you possibly can.

I prefer to dictate directly into Microsoft Word, because I have found this improves my speed threefold. You may type on a computer or tablet, dictate into a recording on your cell phone, or even handwrite your manuscript. Find the method that works best for you.

Create a schedule for writing and stick to it. Make it known to your family and friends that you are not to be disturbed while you're writing for any reason except dire emergencies. Turn off the cell phone, stay away from Facebook, don't answer emails, eliminate Internet interruptions, ensure the TV is turned off or, better yet, in a different room, and spend your time writing and doing nothing else.

Another good idea is to set a word or page count goal. I set a goal of a minimum of 5,000 words a day, five days a week. Keep in mind that you must perform all the other tasks associated with your self-publishing career such as promotion, public speaking, book signings, and so forth. Be sure that your goals are not so aggressive that you can't accomplish these other tasks.

When you're first starting out, 5,000 words a day is probably not attainable, but as you become more comfortable with writing you'll find it becomes easier and easier.

In other words, and generally speaking, don't set unchallenging goals, but also don't set yourself up for failure by setting your targets so high that you can't reach them on a consistent basis. Constantly failing is not good for one's self-esteem.

PUBLISH

There's a lot more to publishing a book than writing it and slapping a cover on it. — **Vince Flynn**

If you're going to self-publish, you must learn the process of publishing. There are many ways to self-publish. Some of them, such as Amazon's KDP (Kindle) and CreateSpace (Paperback), Smashwords and Draft2Digital let you publish your books without charge. I highly recommend that you take the time to learn how to do these publishing steps yourself. Once you've gone through the process a few times, it becomes simple and straightforward.

There are companies who will charge you a fee to publish your book for you. They often bundle many other services such as promotion, marketing, formatting, and so forth into the package to make it appear more attractive. Get and verify references, and search for reviews online to get an idea of

Chapter 1
The Basics

how they have performed in the past. While many of these companies are honest, some will underperform and overprice their products.

There is no reason why you can't perform the publishing steps yourself. It can be challenging, especially the first or second time through, but if you do it yourself, you'll be able to make changes later without having to call someone else to do it for you.

Before you undertake publishing your book, get it proofread by someone else, preferably a professional. Any time you make any significant changes, get it proofread again.

You'll also need a book cover, all the information on the book page on Amazon, and people who will review your book in exchange for a free copy. It's best to get the commitment of at least a dozen individuals to write a review within a week of the publication date of your book.

I know that seems like a lot of steps, but after the first few times through the process you'll find it gets easier. Sometimes the problem is that there are a lot of small steps, as opposed to a few large ones. To simplify, create a checklist of everything that you need to do to get a book published in the order that it needs to be done.

Maintain a Blog

> *Don't focus on having a great blog. Focus on producing a blog that's great for your readers.* — **Brian Clark**

If you're going to be a professional author, you must create and maintain a blog. This is because you need a place on the web that you can call your home, where all the information about you and your books is centralized.

By doing this, you can inform people from within your email signature, business cards, contracts, your books, and elsewhere where to find more information about you, where to sign up for your email list, and how to contact you.

Having a blog makes this simple: you just tell them to go to your blog.

Build an Email List

> *An email without clarity is like an annoying mime: Just say what you want or get out the way!* — **Jordie van Rijn**

One of your primary intentions as you move forward should be to get people to sign up to your email list. This allows you to send out notifications to a dedicated group of fans whenever you'd like. By owning and maintaining an email list, you will increase your profits and keep your fan base engaged.

If you don't actively build and maintain your email list, you are leaving money on the table.

Chapter 1
The Basics

SOCIAL MEDIA

> *Whether via social media or in person, building your relationships is a long-term process, and the ultimate goal is to strengthen your network one person at a time.* — **Raymond Arroyo**

Many people are tempted to use social media as their primary promotional method. After all, it seems so easy to post all about your brand-new book and why it's the best thing since sliced bread.

The problem with using social media is that it is usually used incorrectly. Social media is a great way to build relationships with your readers, which will, over time, lead to improved sales. Just remember it's not a sales tool and shouldn't be used that way.

This will also be discussed more in more detail later, but one thing that you want to avoid is the "buy my book" kind of advertisement or post to your social media. These tend to be very ineffective and serve to push away your readers[3]. Instead, you should write short articles or paragraphs of interest to your audience, and then just mention your book casually or include a link in your tagline.

Social media must be a part of your daily routine, and it needs to be done correctly to be effective. Executed incorrectly, all it will accomplish will be alienate readers and take up valuable time with no results.

---

[3] Constantly posting advertising or "buy my book" type posts may even get your Facebook or other social media account "frozen" for a short time or even closed entirely.

PROMOTE AND MARKET

> *Without promotion, something terrible happens... nothing! — **P. T. Barnum***

One of the big truths about creating a product of any kind – and it's especially true about self-published books – is that they don't sell themselves. This often comes as a surprise to many new authors who spend months, or even years, writing a masterpiece only to find that they sell a dozen copies to their friends and family – and that's it.

Inevitably, the problem is a lack of promotion. This is a very large subject, and entire courses and volumes of books have been written about it. At this point in time, suffice to say that if you don't promote your books, they won't sell.

Promotion can be as simple as posting articles about the subject of the book to your social media, or as complex as buying ads in newspapers, newsletters, and on the web.

We'll be discussing promotion and marketing in much more detail throughout this book.

OUTSOURCE

> *If you deprive yourself of outsourcing and your competitors do not, you're putting yourself out of business. — **Lee Kuan Yew***

As discussed previously, there are many moving parts involved in the creation of a published book. You must write the book, edit and proofread the manuscript, market and promote yourself and your books, maintain a blog, create book covers, write book descriptions, and so forth.

There are a lot of tasks to perform, and you probably don't have the skills or time to do them all yourself.

That's where a concept called outsourcing comes into play. This is the ability to use other people to do some of the work for you. For example, visit a site called Fiverr.com and you'll find contractors who will do small tasks such as designing a book cover, writing an Amazon book description, designing a webpage, or even writing a press release. On this site, you'll find some good rates and, with a little experimentation, can generally locate some talented people to do useful work for you.

Note

The Writing King offers consulting services to help writers with every phase of writing, publishing and marketing their books. Visit our web site for more information.

https://www.theghostwritingking.com

By intelligently utilizing the concept of outsourcing, you can increase the amount of work that you get done by several times.

Exercise – Visit Fiverr.com and examine the various gigs (offers to do work) that are available. Look for those that might prove helpful to your writing career.

CONCLUSIONS

Being a self-published author is one of the most fulfilling and interesting ways for a creative person to make a living. The writing life, as it is sometimes called, means that you get to work from home, which implies that you have more time to spend with your family and friends.

You must understand, though, that there is far more to making a living as a self-published author than just writing words and publishing books.

The rest of this manuscript will go into the various areas that you need to cover on a regular basis to move from being a writer who sells a dozen copies to friends and family, to becoming a professional, self-published, income-earning author.

Chapter 2
What to Write

Before I became a writer, I was a computer security expert, and had gone through several specialized training courses on how to keep the bad guys out of computers. This is a subject that I'm passionate about – helping people secure their systems so they don't lose their financial data, their photos, and their hard work.

Because of this passion, I decided the first book that I was going to tackle was about how to keep a home computer safe on the Internet. I spent about six months writing that book, carefully reviewing it about a dozen times to make sure it was as perfect as I could make it. I hired an artist to create humorous drawings to lighten the mood, paid a professional to create a book cover, and promoted it everywhere that I could find.

The book sold less than 10 copies within a month. By then I'd already published my second book, again on a subject that I was passionate about – surviving disasters. The story was the same with that manuscript – I spent several months researching, writing, and promoting it with very few sales.

I was perplexed but not defeated. After taking a few courses, I realized what was wrong.

I wrote these first two books about my own passions, but I didn't take the time to determine if other people were interested in those subjects.

By then, I started to work for a company called LinkedIn Makeover. My job was to write LinkedIn profiles for executives and others to showcase their skills and talents. I became passionate about writing

33

Chapter 2
What to Write

these profiles and making sure that my clients were shown in the best possible light on that social media network. I decided this might be a good topic for a book, and spent some time determining if other people would be interested in the subject.

After about a month of writing, and some good promotion, the book sold over 5,000 copies in its first two months. In fact, it got up to number 43 on the list of top sellers of all Kindle books for three days.

The lesson I learned is to write about what other people want to read enough to purchase a book about the subject. In other words, figure out other people's passions and write about those things.

It can be extremely frustrating to write a book which doesn't sell. Sometimes, no matter what you do, it seems that nobody wants to buy it. It's important not to take this personally. There is always a good reason why a book is not selling.

It may be that the cover is not attractive enough, the book description doesn't entice your customers, or the "look inside" only contains copyright information and not a sample of the writing. Your book could be in the wrong category, have poorly chosen keywords, or be competing with other books that are much higher in the rankings.

One reason why a book won't sell is that the subject is not popular. In other words, there are few, if any, buyers.

Indeed, a book on different ways to peel potatoes might be of interest to you, but you may have trouble finding people who want to pay money to read what you've written. There are some subjects that are so unpopular that people won't even accept free downloads for their Kindle.

I have found the most popular books that I've written have been created at an intersection of my knowledge, skills and passions with other people's desires, passions, and needs.

It can be difficult to write about a subject that you don't know or care about. Research can solve that problem, but this obviously adds more time and complexity to writing a book. It is always a multiple win when you learn deeply about yet another subject.

Nevertheless, it is always advisable and promising to write about a topic you have had some direct and personal experience with, because only in this way will you be able to bring the necessary facts and research alive through deep awareness and experience.

Because of this, one of the first steps to figuring out what to write about is to understand your own passions, knowledge, skills, goals, and desires.

Exercise: Get a piece of paper and spend a few minutes writing down a list of your passions, experiences, knowledge and skills. Don't overcomplicate this exercise – keep it quick and to the point.

For example, my list is as follows:

Passions: Human Rights; Writing; Photography

Skills: Computer security; management, leadership; writing; photography

Knowledge: American history; the Roman Empire

Experiences: Bullied in school; Trip across the southwest; Hiking in Joshua Tree; Being manager and leader; Going on a cruise; Being married; Caring for chronically ill person for 8 years

Take the time to make this kind of list for yourself. Don't worry about whether these topics will sell – we'll get to that later.

WHAT YOU KNOW

I was coaching a friend of mine recently about her writing. She wanted to become an author, but had no idea what to write about. She'd been stumped for weeks, racking her brain to try and figure out good subjects for books.

As we talked on the phone, I started asking questions about her life. Did she have challenges going to school? Was she bullied? Is she the go-to person for something in her group of friends? Does she love doing something, like gardening? Is she religious? Does she respect somebody famous and know all about them?

Asking these questions dissolved some of the blocks she was feeling and she realized there were many topics that she could explore with her writing. She finally settled on writing a book about how to help children with disabilities – it seemed that she'd been doing that for a long time.

Everyone has skills, experience, and knowledge about one or more subjects. Sometimes this can be simple, such as how to color a picture so that it looks good. Other times it can be complex, such as different ways to optimally organize a modern, computerized factory floor.

The first step towards becoming a self-published author is to determine what you can write about.

I'll go over a few things from my own life, which might give you some context on how to do this.

As with most people, I had varied experiences in childhood, and learned many lessons as I was growing up. Any number of these could serve as subjects for a book. For example, I had a bully who beat me up every single day on the way home from school, and finally I had to deal with that problem myself. That's a great topic for a book and it would be very helpful to many young people.

Also, I remember how frustrated I was with my parents as I was growing up. They didn't seem to understand the problems I was having, and clearly communicated that theirs were far more important than mine. How does a child deal with this? This is another great topic for a book for young people.

Looking forward through my life, I became a computer programmer – writing applications –, then a manager, a leader of a small group, and then a large one. Each of these different areas of life presented obstacles that I overcame, which other people might be interested in learning to do as well.

Skills are another area to look at. For example, I am a skilled computer programmer, computer security expert, photographer, and writer. I've been trained in each of these areas, have made significant money performing these specialties, and have mastered them to a certain degree.

Chapter 2
What to Write

I could write one or more books about any of those areas in which I'm skilled. For example, I photographed women for eight years and became experienced about how to pose them for the best possible picture. There you have a great topic for a book.

One of my passions is history, especially the Roman Empire, World War II, and the Cold War. I'm very knowledgeable about these areas due to the number of articles and books that I've read on the subjects. This represents a wealth of information that can be used to write books.

Another area offering an ample wealth of possible book ideas is the people that you've known, admired, or even hated. Perhaps you had a great grandmother who served as a mentor, giving you many life lessons that others could benefit from. For example, my grandfather spent four years in a Japanese prisoner of war camp in World War II – he passed along many experiences and lessons that would be great topics for a book.

If you look back through your own life, and survey and reflect on all your experiences, hobbies, skills, and knowledge, as well as the interesting and influential people who have touched your life, you'll find that you have many topics that you could write about and expand into book form.

This is great place to begin your journey as a self-published author.

- What experiences have influenced and touched you deeply?
- What do you know about well?

- What skills are you adept at?
- Who have you known and loved?
- What hobbies bring you joy?

Exercise: Make a list of potential topics without worrying about whether anybody else is interested in them. You can prune that list down later, but the first thing is to understand that you've learned awesome things, you have unique abilities, you've gone through trials and tribulations, and you've known kick-ass people. These things are potential book topics.

FINDING AN INTERESTING TOPIC

> *Books are to be distinguished by the grandeur of their topics even more than by the manner in which they are treated.* — **Henry David Thoreau**

One of the great things about being a self-published author is that you can write about anything you want. Whatever wild idea comes into your head is fair game, assuming it's not illegal or obscene, as a subject for a book. This freedom to write and publish anything is unprecedented in history, and you should certainly take advantage of the opportunity to make your thoughts, feelings, and knowledge known to others.

Unfortunately, writing and publishing a book, and making money from it are two entirely different things.

Chapter 2
What to Write

There are several points in the creation of your book that are critical for earning a profit as a writer. The first, and arguably the most important point, becomes relevant before you have even begun work on the book.

If you just write about things willy-nilly and publish a book about any random plot that's of interest to you, then more than likely your books are not going to sell very well and they probably won't make much money.

That's why it is of utmost importance that you learn how to research the book's marketplace before you put a single word down into your manuscript. Even a little bit of research can prevent you from spinning your wheels on topics that don't sell any books, and help you to positively focus on ones that can make you some reward.

For example, I'm a computer security expert, and used my skills at Trader Joe's for over twenty years. As I mentioned earlier, the first book that I wrote, without doing any market research at all, was about how to secure your home computer. I was convinced that this would sell well because in my mind, 'who wouldn't want to have a secure computer?'

Much to my surprise, it turns out that people, as a rule, simply are not interested in spending the time or money to lock down their computer system. All they want to do is buy a product. At the most, install it on their computer and forget about it.

Alas, the book didn't sell very well at all. In fact, its profits didn't even cover its own costs. I wasn't discouraged, because by that time I had already published and written several more books, some of which were selling and making some money.

Later, I performed some basic research on moneymaking topics and found that many people were interested in making money while working from home. Because of that, I began writing a series of books on how to do exactly that. Having learned the right lessons, these sold relatively well without heavy promotion.

There are a vast number of ways that you can do research about topics for your fiction or nonfiction books.

LIBRARIES

I spent three days a week for 10 years educating myself in the public library, and it's better than college. People should educate themselves - you can get a complete education for no money. At the end of 10 years, I had read every book in the library and I'd written a thousand stories. — **Ray Bradbury**

How long has it been since you visited your local library? If you don't already know, find out where your local library is located, and cheerfully head on over. You'll be pleasantly surprised at what you'll find. The people who work in your library live and breathe books and you'll find that by talking to them, you can get a good feel for subjects and topics that are popular amongst readers. While you're there, see if there are any writing, or other related groups, that meet occasionally. Then, make it a point to visit them.

Exercise: Visit your local library and discuss possible topics with the librarians. Don't forget to chat with the volunteer workers (often college students) as they will often have a good idea what is currently of interest to people. While you are there, get a library card (if you don't have one already) and make it a point to visit at least once a month. Librarians are great friends to writers and you will find their knowledge and experience invaluable.

BOOKSTORES

> *A bookstore is one of the many pieces of evidence we have that people are still thinking.* — **Jerry Seinfeld**

I'm sure there's at least one or more bookstores in your local area. The people who work in these establishments understand books and know what is selling. They are constantly exposed to the book-buying public – exactly the type of people you are looking for and needing to understand.

Exercise: Visit two local bookstores: a large chain bookstore and a smaller, mom-and-pop establishment. Take a few hours, scan the shelves; see what's selling, talk to the people who work there, and even to some of the patrons. Also, take the time to find out if there any local groups that meet or at least advertise in the bookstore. Make a point of introducing yourself to the manager and assistant manager – they can become great resources as you establish yourself as a local writer.

MEETUPS

If you want to find people who are interested in similar topics, head over to a site which is now ubiquitous and synonymous to the idea: Meetup.com. Join and search for meetups on topics that are of interest. These can be hit or miss, but I found that as a rule, meetup groups are quite a good way to meet people, get into some conversations, and find out what kind of books they're interested in buying. You can almost certainly find several meetup groups within driving distance, about topics of interest to you.

Exercise: Join www.meetup.com if you haven't already, and use their search function to find local writing groups. There is probably one or even more within driving distance. Visit those groups, find one or two whose vibe you like, and become a regular member.

Also, look for groups that match your interests. If you enjoy sewing and knitting, and that's what you want to write about, then find some local groups that do those activities, join them, and become a regular member.

AMAZON

> *We've had three big ideas at Amazon that we've stuck with for 18 years, and they're the reason we're successful: Put the customer first. Invent. And be patient.* — **Jeff Bezos**

Amazon is the largest "book store" in the world, and it will become your primary market when you publish your books. It's important that you understand the tools available to help you as an author.

Go to the Amazon search bar and enter a keyword or phrase describing your book. Search for books with that keyword. For example, if your book is about selling on eBay, enter *'selling on eBay'* into the search bar.

Chapter 2
What to Write

Click on the first book, assuming it is about the correct subject, and scroll to the Product Details section. A sample is shown below.

Product Details

Series: Earn Money from Your Home
Paperback: 132 pages
Publisher: The Writing King (August 4, 2016)
Language: English
ISBN-10: 1943517363
ISBN-13: 978-1943517367
Product Dimensions: 6 x 0.3 x 9 inches
Shipping Weight: 1 6 ounces (View shipping rates and policies)
Average Customer Review: ☆☆☆☆☆ (25 customer reviews)
Amazon Best Sellers Rank: #93,948 in Books (See Top 100 in Books)
    #13 in Books > Computers & Technology > Internet & Social Media > eBay
    #92 in Books > Business & Money > Small Business & Entrepreneurship > Home Based

Look at the field marked "Amazon Best Sellers Rank". This number directly reflects how many copies the book is selling.

Put the number in the "Amazon Sales Rank Calculator" at the following link, and write down the result.

http://smooth.li/salescalc

Now that you know how one book is selling, check out a few more for your keyword or phrase. Once you've located a dozen or so books, change the keyword or phrase to something related, for example 'make money on eBay', and repeat the process.

Next, click on one of the categories in the first book you found. In the above example this is:

Books>Computers & Technology>Internet & Social Media>eBay

Starting from the first book in that category (ignore books that are not related to your topic) repeat the same procedure as above to get the number of sales per week for a dozen or so books.

You can repeat this procedure with other categories to get a good idea of how well your topic is selling.

Once you've searched a half dozen terms and checked a few categories, look at the pattern. Are books on that topic selling 1 copy per week? 20 copies? Hundreds of copies?

If the books you find are selling thousands or tens of thousands of copies, then the keyword or phrase is very competitive. You'll find it difficult to get your book noticed because the better selling books will always be listed ahead of yours.

On the other hand, if you consistently see values of 0 or 1 for dozens of books, that tells you that this topic is a slow seller.

The ideal is to find a topic which sells good numbers (a thousand copies a week) at the top end, but rapidly falls off to a few dozen a week or less. If all your findings are in the thousands, that topic is probably way too competitive for you to do well.

This is a very simple, albeit time consuming, exercise, and many people have come up with other methods.

Kindle Spy automates this process to a certain extent, and will help you get a feel for the difficulty you will likely have trying to sell books in specific categories. The advantage of this product is that it will offer information about Kindle categories such as their competitiveness, popularity, and potential. If these are green on the display, then you have a good chance of writing a book that will sell. Yellow or red in any of them means you got your work cut out for you.

> http://smooth.li/kindlespy
> *Note, this is an affiliate link. If you purchase the product I will receive a small commission.*

Exercise: Spend some time examining the sales statistics of books within your topic/category to find out if they're selling. Search for your subject and select a few books, one at a time. On each book page, look at the Product Details section and find the "Amazon Best Sellers Rank". Follow the procedure described at the beginning of this section to familiarize yourself with book rankings.

FACEBOOK AND OTHER SOCIAL MEDIA

As an author, you should be very active on social media outlets such as Facebook, Google Plus, Pinterest, Instagram, LinkedIn, and Goodreads at the least. Join groups that pertain to your topics, and spend some time getting into online conversations with people in those groups about their interests and likelihood of purchasing books on certain subjects. You'll begin to learn what is selling and what isn't from these conversations. Keep in mind that your purpose is only to do research and avoid the temptation to try to sell your own books.

Exercise: Get into a few conversations on social media about book topics and subjects of interest to you as an author. Search for groups about your topics, join, and take part in conversations. Over the long time, you should be doing this on a regular basis (several times a week) to build a fan base of interested readers.

CONCLUSIONS

I think you can see the common thread through most of these methods of research. The best idea is to get out there and interact with people, see what's on bookshelves, look in the libraries and see what they're renting out, and look at statistics on sites such as Amazon.

None of this is perfect and there are no guarantees that your book will sell. There are other variables such as the quality of your cover, how well your book description is written, your title, subtitle, the state of the economy, the season of the year, and so forth. Some of these are within your control – you can change your cover for example – and some of them aren't.

The point is that by performing even some rudimentary research upfront, you can reduce the possibility that you'll spend an ungodly amount of time writing, editing, proofreading, publishing, promoting, and marketing a book that's not going to sell because it's a weak niche or possibly because there's not a market for it.

Of course, if you write and publish books quickly, and have many them in your portfolio, then a weak selling volume won't do any harm. But if you only have one or two books to sell, then yes – poor sales can be a big problem.

Chapter 3
Writing

> *It's amazing how many people call themselves writers yet, don't write. Honestly, to be a professional writer of any kind, much less to make a living publishing your own books, you must write every single day.*

It goes without saying that if you're going to be a self-published author, you must write books. Well, that's not totally true in all cases. It is possible to hire ghostwriters to do the work of writing, but that's outside of the scope of this manuscript. Our focus here is only on writers who self-publish their own works.

As I said, to be an author, you must write. It doesn't matter what gets in the way — writer's block, malicious people with critical comments, grammar Nazis, family, friends, emergencies, and everything else — you must find time to write.

I block out about 50% of my work time every day to spend writing. The other 50% is split between other tasks such as promotion, publishing, networking, and so forth. The reason for this is that I'm a writer, and the primary characteristic of a writer is writing.

Exercise: For one or more days, keep a notebook with you and note down everything you do. Be sure to include work, play, travel (including commuting), time with the kids and family, TV watching, video game playing, goofing around, and everything else. Don't make any evaluations about anything – just note what you did and the time spent.

Once you've got a list (three days is best to catch a wide spectrum and cross-section of activities) examine it and determine which activities are required and which are optional. With that information, could you create enough time during the day to write? You'll need at least 4 hours a day. Work out what you can do to increase your writing time.

CHOOSE YOUR WRITING TOOLS

A mechanic needs a box full of wrenches, air guns, and other tools. An artist might need paintbrushes and paints, while a sculptor needs a hammer and chisel. In the same light, a writer needs something to write with, probably a computer of some kind, a word processor, possibly dictation software, and other tools. For a professional career, your tools need to be of the highest quality that you can find – otherwise, you'll be fighting them instead of writing.

How will you do your writing? Do you prefer handwriting, using a typewriter, typing into a computer, or speaking the words into your word processor? Maybe you prefer talking to a recording device and transcribing that into digital form. According to an interview, *50 Shades of Grey* was written on a Blackberry (Ferreras 2015), and I'm sure many books have been written on iPads, smartphones, or other devices.

Whatever tool you choose for writing, make sure that it works well for you. Using the incorrect tools, poor applications, slow

Chapter 3
Writing

computers, and so forth will slow you down, make you frustrated, and might lead to writer's block.

I use the Dragon line of dictation software to speak my writing directly into Microsoft Word 2016. Microsoft Word is fully featured, and includes excellent built-in grammar and spell-checking.

For travelling, I bought an inexpensive Google Chromebook. It cost less than $300, is lightning fast, and supports many applications over the web. It's enough to get the writing done, without all the distracting bells and whistles.

The advantage of using dictation software is that most people talk several times faster than they can type. For example, I can type between 1,500 and 2,000 words per hour, but I can dictate as many as 2,000 to 4,000 words per hour. Of course, in both cases, I need to read through what I've written to edit out any mistakes.

As a writer, your word processor, computer (or smartphone, iPad, or even Blackberry) and email system are your most important physical tools. If they are slow or crash often, you will lose productivity, which means your writing will be slower and you will be frustrated and unhappy.

It is therefore vital that you choose a word processor and computing resources that are fast, don't crash, and help, rather than hinder your writing.

If you enjoy very rudimentary approaches, like a typewriter or the back-to-basics, pen and paper, simply make sure it is the most efficient and enjoyable way for you to write.

Chapter 3
Writing

Make sure your word processor has an excellent built-in grammar and spell-checker. You shouldn't totally depend on these, but they can help reduce the number of errors that pop up in your writing. This is especially important if you use dictation software, because the automatic grammar and spell-checker can fix many dictation errors.

If you can't afford a good word processor, you can use Microsoft Office 365 online or Google docs. Office 365 online is far superior in functionality compared to Google docs, but both are free and do an excellent job.

http://office365.com

http://docs.google.com

A huge advantage of using the online versions (either Google Docs or Office 365) is that your documents are stored in the cloud and not on your computer. Thus, if your system crashes, your documents will be unaffected. Additionally, you can edit them from any computer that can access the web.

The main disadvantage of Microsoft Office 365 online is that Dragon will not allow you to dictate directly into the web-based word processor, but it does provide a small "Dragon Pad" that accepts your dictation, which you can then copy and paste into your document.

Google docs comes with a built-in dictation application which is very fast and accurate. If you use this, you won't need to purchase Dragon.

Exercise: Spend some time checking out both Office 365 online and Google docs. If you don't have one already, create an account on each, and compare them by functionality and speed. You might be able to avoid spending any money by using one of these applications, assuming they are fast enough to keep up with your writing.

YOUR WRITING ROUTINE

> *As a writer, I have found the statement "watch your back" to be especially profound. Writers tend to sit all day long typing or dictating to the computer, and that's very hard on the back. It's important to build time away from your writing into your workday to protect your health, your back and even your mental state.*

One of the problems that writers have is that they sit in a chair for many hours at a time, typing on a keyboard or talking into a microphone. This can lead to obesity, health problems, backaches, knee pain, headaches, and a host of other issues. It can also make a writer irritable and argumentative.

To alleviate these problems, write for a certain amount of time, say 45 minutes, and then get up and do something physically active for 15 minutes or so.

I set a timer by my desk for 45 minutes, and write for that amount of time. When the timer dings, I get up and take a walk, make lunch, go out on the deck and stare into space, or anything else other than writing.

My chiropractor recommended doing this to help with back pain. It works like a charm, and I find it interesting that working for several hours in a row is less productive than taking a 15-minute break every 45 minutes.

Exercise: In the morning, write for three hours without taking a break. Take a break for lunch, and then in the afternoon, write for 45 minutes and take a 15-minute break three times in a row.

Afterwards, take note the differences in how you felt about your productivity while practicing each of these two methods.

YOUR VOICE AND STYLE

You are unique and you have your own viewpoint and style. Instead of trying to emulate every other author out there, work on your uniqueness and communicate your messages in your style. That's how you'll become a great writer.

The most important thing you need to do once you decide to become a self-published author is to find your voice and style. This fact is true for any kind of artist, whether they are painters, sculptors, writers, pottery makers, weavers, and even actors and actresses.

You can be taught the mechanics of writing, but only experience will guide you to the creation of your own point of view, style, and voice. Once you break out of the mundane sameness you were taught in formalized courses, your writing career will really start to take off.

Besides, you'll feel a lot more satisfied writing books from your heart. You'll find that once you master putting out your own viewpoint and style, writing becomes a joy and you'll look forward to those times that you spend transforming your thoughts into book form.

How do you bring out these qualities in your writing? It starts from one simple statement:

Write.

You must write consistently and constantly, for several hours every day.

Exercise: Everyone is passionate about something in their life. Write a one page essay that is somehow related to your passion. Don't worry about spelling, grammar, or style. Just write it.

Next, write a page about something you understand but doesn't generate any passion in your heart.

Compare the two. Notice any differences in the way they read? Which one is better? Which one did you enjoy writing more?

WRITING EVERY DAY

> *Are you writing for several hours each day? That's one of the marks of a professional versus an amateur – a professional will find the time to write regardless of what's happening. An amateur will give in to excuses.*

As I've said before, to be a writer, you must write. That might seem to be a no-brainer, but it needs to be said and repeated because quite a few people say they are writers or authors but have trouble sitting down and getting their words into a manuscript, whether it be digital, typed, or handwritten.

There are many other things to accomplish to get your works ready for publication, including finding an audience, marketing to that audience, publishing your books, and so forth, but the long and short of it is – this is worth repeating at infinitum – that to be a writer you must write.

The best way to learn to write is to do it a lot and to get critique from your peers on what you've written. If you're going to be a professional in this field you generally should be writing several thousands of words at a minimum every single day.

I know, I know. I can hear you voicing your objections. Some of you are telling yourselves that I'm crazy or don't understand the situation. You might say you don't have time to write that much due to work and family life. You could tell me that you feel fortunate if you can get a couple of hundred words written.

You could even say that a goal of, say, two thousand words a day, or even a week, is unrealistic, especially for you in your circumstances. How can anyone write that much and still take care of their other responsibilities?

An interesting fact of life is that people put energy into what's important to them. Conversely, if an activity is unimportant, then people will not put in the requisite time and energy to be successful in that area.

This fact presents an easy way to tell the importance of something to someone: they will put in the time, effort, and energy into that activity. You can use this information to separate what is real or factual from what they are just saying.

If you believe that your writing is important, for whatever reason, then devote the time, energy and effort necessary to become a professional.

Writing is not an easy occupation, and trying to make a living as a self-published author is even more difficult, if only because you also need to learn and master so many other specialties.

Before you begin the journey of becoming a writer in the real sense of the word, ask yourself if you're willing to put in the time and effort to make it happen.

I'll reiterate; to succeed, the primary thing that you need to do, day in and day out, every single day of the week, is write as many words as you can.

Exercise: Write a one page essay or story in an area where you feel impassioned. In other words, if you love (or think you'll love) mystery writing, then write a quick mystery. Once you are finished, describe how you feel.

SET A QUOTA FOR EACH DAY

Set a daily word quota you will commit to writing each day. Your target should be attainable but not easy. Over time, gradually increase your word target and keep challenging yourself.

I found that the best way to ensure that I write enough each day is to set a goal or quota in the morning for how many words I'm going to complete by the time the day is over.

When I get up I look at my calendar and see what is scheduled —I also do ghostwriting, blogging, and other services for clients – and set a quota based upon how many hours are left in the day. I make it a point to write at least four hours each day, and complete at least 1,000 words an hour (by complete I mean dictated and reviewed twice).

A good rule is to allocate at least 50% of the workable time in a day towards writing self-published books. Publishing, promoting, and all the other tasks, including those needed for paying clients, take up the other 50%.

My standard word quota for each day is 5,000 words for the books that I am personally authoring. I can easily write 10,000 words in a single day, every day of the week, but I found that it's best to ensure that what I write is ready for the proofreader by the time the day is finished. That way I don't have to confront a very large number of words that need to be edited and proofread all at once.

Exercise: In the morning, when you get up, set a quota for how much you will write that day. Meet that quota. Was it overwhelming, or a walk in the park? Find a challenging medium and adjust as needed.

WRITE THEN EDIT

Do you enjoy writer's block, getting frustrated and low productivity? Me neither. Don't write and edit at the same time. That only slows you down.

One of the best ways to slow down your pace and introduce writer's block is to edit at the same time as you write. When you write, you must simply write. Don't keep going back to re-edit the same line or paragraph over and over.

Many authors don't understand that the purpose of the first draft is merely to get your thoughts down into your manuscript in some semblance of order. There is no need for it to be publishable, polished, or even readable.

You know how it goes: write a sentence, review that sentence, rewrite a word or two, review it again, rewrite a few more words, review again, delete the whole thing, write it again, and, after a while you may then find yourself stuck and unable to write.

Don't do that. Instead, type or dictate the words as quickly as you can and don't look back – until later.

The concept is to get your ideas and words out of your head and onto the page or digital paper. Editing while you are writing slows down this process to a crawl. If you do it too much, writer's block will rear its ugly head and you'll find yourself unable to proceed.

Once you've written a certain amount of text, then go back and make a pass to edit it and make it more readable. My practice is to write an entire chapter, using voice dictation, and then go back and edit that chapter separately.

You'll find that keeping these two tasks makes authoring a book go much quicker because writing requires a whole different set of skills than editing.

Exercise: Write a one page essay about any subject and edit it as you go along. When you are finished with that, write another page without editing, then go back and edit it afterwards. Did you notice any difference?

WRITING JOURNAL

Keeping a writing journal is a great way to hone your writing skills. These journals are used to record your thoughts, ideas and concepts and are not meant to be published.

It's quite common for an author to keep a writer's journal with them everywhere they go. This is usually a notebook and is usually handwritten.

A writer's journal is a good idea because you can jot down notes, phrases, ideas, concepts, or thoughts wherever you happen to be at the time.

I've never been too attracted to the idea of a writing journal because my mind doesn't work that way. My style is to sit down in front of a computer for blocks of time – a whole morning, afternoon, or evening - and keep writing until I've met my minimum word count or time goal for the day at the very least. If I feel very motivated, then I continue writing past my goal. However, regardless of how I feel, the goal must be met.

On the other hand, some authors keep meticulous notes throughout the day of anything that pops into their head. I've known several who fill up huge notebooks with their inspirations, various and rambling thoughts.

Regardless of whether you use a writing journal or not, do keep notes of ideas for stories, books or articles. If you don't do this, you'll kick yourself when you can't quite remember the brilliant idea that came to you in the middle of the night or while walking in the park.

A writing journal can be an awesome tool and it can help you build your writing skills. Just remember, you probably won't be using the words in your journals for your books, promotional materials, and other publishable works, so it should not be counted as part of your quota for the day.

Exercise: Use your notebook, or get another one, and keep it with you for a week. Write down your thoughts, ideas, and so forth whenever you can, and at the end of the week look over what you have done. Is a writing journal something that helps you or is it unnecessary?

Chapter 3
Writing

LEARNING TO WRITE

> *Education can teach you the basics of writing, although it can only go so far.*

You're probably wondering at this point when I'm going to share the secret of how to learn to actually write.

On a formal and obvious level, there are many opportunities to learn the craft of writing. Classes are always available at your local colleges, universities, and trade schools, as well as the obvious online sources, in the form of webinars and tutorials, which can have the advantage of being more personalized.

Some of these classes and courses have good value in that they educate you on the mechanics you'll need, such as grammar, spelling, structure, formatting, and so forth. They may also go into other subjects such as how to promote your work, find an audience, or beef up your social media.

You should explore options for learning writing basics, but keep in mind that although the typical college course on creative writing can teach you a few things about how to write, it tends to channel creativity into specific, "safe" and normal areas and formats.

For example, if you take a college course about writing mystery stories, you're going to learn how to write a standard, soup to nuts mystery including the basics of plot, structure, characters, and so forth. There is value in learning in this manner.

By the end of that class you'll be able to write the exact same type of mystery story that everyone else is publishing. The problem with that is that it churns out the predictable, which is great if your sights are aimed at the safe and average, but not so good if you want to sell a lot of self-published books or become a bestselling mystery author. To achieve those higher goals, your writing must stand out and outshine the competition. The best way to do that is to inject yourself – your unique viewpoint, style, and so forth – into your writing.

On the other hand, you should be constantly learning and taking as many courses as you can afford. Visit Udemy.com for an excellent selection of short, highly focused classes which don't cost an arm and a leg.

I've also found that junior colleges are an inexpensive and accessible method to get the basics that you'll need to succeed. You can also find a few online courses that can help, but be careful because, as I've mentioned before, there are many scams in the wild world of the web.

Some recommended courses and links include:

UDEMY COURSES
Udemy offers tens of thousands of short courses, often less than an hour long, on focused subjects. You'll find just about everything you want here. Udemy frequently runs specials with course prices as low as $10, so be sure to get on their mailing list to take advantage of their specials.

http://smooth.li/udemy
Note, this is an affiliate link. If you purchase the product I will receive a small commission.

Chapter 3
Writing

AUTHOR AUDIENCE ACADEMY
Produced by Shelley Hitz, this series of courses is an outstanding example of a soup to nuts approach to writing, publishing and promoting nonfiction eBooks. Highly recommended.

http://smooth.li/aaa
Note, this is an affiliate link. If you purchase the product I will receive a small commission

STANFORD ADVENTURES IN WRITING
A series of courses presented as a series of graphic novels. This is an interesting way to teach – try it out.

http://smooth.li/stanford

FREE ONLINE CREATIVE WRITING COURSES
This website lists free online courses which are available from various colleges and universities.

http://smooth.li/courses

PURDUE WRITING LAB
An excellent website containing references on writing. This is an invaluable resource.

http://smooth.li/purdue

This list should give you a good start on your writing education.

Tip

Avoid spending $9,997, $99 or $19,999.99 for the slick-sounding training that you learned about after sitting through a 2-hour webinar. Instead, use a fraction of that money to purchase exactly what you need from Udemy, your local community college, free online courses from universities and colleges, or focused, low-cost training, pinpointed to specific subjects.

Exercise: Visit each of the links above and read through the descriptions of the courses. Sign up for one or two courses (don't overdo it) and take them.

WRITING CRITIQUE GROUPS

Once you've been writing a while and have received some training, you'll need to have your work critiqued. Look in your local area or online for writing critique groups.

Once you've learned the basics of writing, perhaps by taking a few courses at your local junior college or online, your best bet for honing your writing skills is to join and attend as many writing critique groups as you can. These are generally informal get-togethers which occur on a weekly, biweekly or monthly basis where writers read one or two chapters from their works and then the other writers in the group provide critique.

Chapter 3
Writing

It is important to understand that critique is not criticism. Per the dictionary (Merriam-Webster.com), criticism is:

> *to express disapproval of (someone or something): to talk about the problems or faults of (someone or something)*

> *to look at and make judgments about (something, such as a piece of writing or a work of art)*

On the other hand, critique is:

> *a careful judgment in which you give your opinion about the good and bad parts of something (such as a piece of writing or a work of art)*

Malicious individuals gain pleasure from criticizing art and writing. Critical remarks are not helpful, and are often intended to cause harm. Your best bet is to ignore them and move on with your life.

On the other hand, critique is used to improve the quality of your writing. To be useful, critique must be specific and actionable. This is one of the primary differences between critique and criticism. Criticism tends to be general without specifics and provides no 'maps' to betterment.

The purpose of writing groups is to give and receive useful and usable feedback on various aspects of your writing.

Some critique groups focus on grammar and punctuation, others are more interested in plot points, characterization and technology. Visit several groups as a guest, until you find one or two that you're comfortable with, and then attend as often as possible.

To find groups, join and use Meetup.com. In most areas, you'll find several groups if you search for "writing groups" or "writing critique groups." I found that groups that meet weekly or every other week work best. Monthly meetings just aren't often enough to extract enough guidance.

http://www.meetup.com

You'll find that these critique groups can be extremely useful in helping you mold your books – or other forms of writing – into a finished, readable work.

For example, I run a weekly critique group which specializes in science-fiction stories. Recently, the feedback that I received regarding a novel that I'm writing is that a character seemed to change personalities from chapter to chapter. It made the book uneven and difficult to read. This was good critique, and by using that input, I rewrote a few paragraphs and made the character much more believable.

My recommendation is to attend as many critique groups as you can fit into your schedule. One or two a week is a good minimum, and the advice you gain will help you bring out your unique qualities and improve your writing.

Exercise: Join Meetup.com if you are not already a member and search for writing critique groups in your area. If you find one or some that inspire you, make the time to attend, and bring along a few pages from one of your works. Do a reading, listen to the critique from others, and when others read, give them great critique as well.

DICTATING

> *Not everyone enjoys dictating their works into their word processor. However, you can double (or more) your writing speed by using voice dictation.*

People tend to speak much faster than they can write, so it makes sense that dictating your words using a product such as Dragon Professional or Google Voice will tend to speed things up.

Voice recognition used to be very primitive and problematic, but the kinks have been worked out of this technology and it now works exceptionally well.

I personally can dictate an entire fifteen-thousand-word book in a single day using Dragon Professional. Of course, another day is required to edit that document into a publishable form, but that's going to be needed regardless of how you get the thoughts down into a manuscript.

Demonstration videos are available on the Nuance (the makers of Dragon Professional) website.

http://smooth.li/dragondemo

If you use Google Docs, you'll find an option called "Voice typing..." under the tools menu of a document.

Additionally, Windows and Apple both have their own built-in voice dictation tools.

There are two methods for using dictation. I prefer to speak the words into the microphone and have them appear in my Word document at the same time. Others dictate into a recording device and then transcribe that recording later. You can find transcribers on Fiverr.com, or use the services from Rev.com or similar sites.

http://Rev.com

All these methods are perfectly acceptable and the one you use depends upon your own personal choice.

Regardless of whether you dictate your words into your manuscript, or whether you write it out using a keyboard, you'll need to make an editing pass or two after you are done.

I like to write, or in my case dictate, a full chapter, then go back and edit that chapter. This alleviates the barrier of having an entire book to edit all at once when I'm done. How much you write before you edit is up to you, but the minimum amount is probably a chapter.

PROOFREADING

Before you publish your book, make sure you have it proofread by yourself (at least twice) and another person, preferably a professional proofreader.

Once you've written or dictated and edited your book, it needs to be proofread for grammar and spelling errors. Ideally, you should do this at several points in your process of writing your book.

Chapter 3
Writing

I typically dictate and review a chapter, then read the entire chapter out loud. It's amazing how many errors are caught using this method.

This might sound like a lot of work, but it's not as bad as it seems on the surface. Dictating a 2,000-word chapter takes me less than an hour. Reviewing that chapter requires perhaps another thirty minutes, and then a proofreading pass are another thirty on top of that. At that point, the chapter is in good condition.

Once I've completed the writing, reviewing and proofreading for the day, I'll go back and read the entire work that I did that day, from beginning to end, out loud.

The idea is that by the time the day is finished, I have several chapters or sections in very good condition.

Once the entire book has been completed, I do one final proofreading pass from beginning to end. This pass is also done out loud, as in my experience that is the best way to catch errors.

Even after all this editing and proofreading, grammar and spelling errors will still manage to squeak by. It is a good idea to get someone else to look over your manuscript for errors for that final polish.

Check out Fiverr.com for very low-cost proofreaders. Better still, you can exchange services with other writers that you know (you proofread each other's works). This is one of the advantages of building your writing network.

Another place to look is FindAProofreader.com. You can search their database of over 200 proofreaders, ask for quotes, and compare prices.

> http://findaproofreader.com/

There are tools such as Grammarly and Autocrit which can help you find spelling, grammar, and even contextual errors. Grammarly is easier to use, but Autocrit has far more options and better reporting.

> http://smooth.li/grammarly
> *Note, this is an affiliate link. If you purchase the product I will receive a small commission.*

> http://smooth.li/autocrit

Use Grammarly for non-fiction and Autocrit for fiction.

Another great site is GrammerBase.com. This service is free.

> http://www.grammarbase.com/

Take advantage of the tools that are built into your word processor, such as Microsoft Word, to check for basic grammar and spelling errors. I've found the grammar and spell-checking within Microsoft Word 365 and 2016 are excellent; the previous versions were substandard in quality.

Exercise: Write a one page essay on any subject. Read it through out loud and correct any errors. Now go to Fiverr.com and find a proofreader. Submit your essay (it will probably cost $5 to $20 depending upon the length). Once it comes back, usually in a few days, examine the results and note how many corrections were made. While waiting for the proofreader at Fiverr.com to check your document, go to GrammarBase.com, submit your essay, and save the results. Compare this with the work done by the proofreader at Fiverr.com

INVALIDATIONS AND CRITICISM

> *It is inevitable that people will make evaluations about the quality and content of your works. And no matter how good it is, there will be a certain amount of invalidation and criticism. Be careful to not let those comments get in your way.*

Something you must be careful about throughout your writing career, but especially during educational times, is the people who invalidate or criticize your writing.

Writers and artists frequently get attacked by insecure and malicious individuals in society – these are haters for the most part. This is especially true on the Internet on sites such as YouTube and Facebook, but it can happen anywhere.

When I was in high school, my English teacher read one of my short stories and told me that I'd never be a writer. He said my work was boring, mundane, predictable, and difficult to understand. Those comments were exceptionally discouraging since I trusted him as an authority and this contributed to my failure to move into professional writing at that time in my life.

An evaluation can be as subtle as a shrug and a frown after reading a chapter, a biting, sarcastic remark, or a lack-luster comment such as "it was okay". These seemingly minor criticisms can have quite an impact on an author or artist. Primarily, this is due to the general nature of the comments — there's nothing that can be done, barring a complete rewrite, to rectify the supposed flaws that were implied.

The best strategy is to ignore this type of criticism.

Often these comments are not meant to be malicious. Perhaps someone is having a bad day, has a headache, or simply hasn't had their coffee yet. Don't antagonize them; just ignore their comments.

Critical remarks can come from anyone; family, friend, or foe. Heck, it can even come from an inexpert source or one whose support and admiration has never been lacking. One never knows what deeper reasons may provoke these negative slurs.

Often, I've found that temporary writer's block is the direct result of negativity. Subtle remarks can be the most damaging because they are not always noticed at the time they are said. Instead, these words tend to get buried in the mind, and surface later as growing barriers or insecurities. This invalidating effect can be magnified because the comments are often strategic or sly and on some level, meant to cut down.

Be especially wary when reading comments on social media. People can get quite vicious when commenting about books or other creative endeavors and the remarks can be extremely upsetting and discouraging.

Chapter 3
Writing

For some odd reason, this is especially true of the comments left on YouTube videos. I've found it's a good idea to avoid reading these comments. Turn off the commenting if you can. I've found through experience that there is very little to gain by leaving your YouTube post open to comments.

Never reply to totally negative and unconstructive comments. Never contact the commenter to argue, try to get them to change their mind, or even to solicit more information or feedback. In these cases, it is not worth the trouble. You are probably going to open the proverbial can-of-worms by getting in contact and you probably have better things to do with your time.

When someone has left a negative comment on one of my works I make a point to delete it as soon as possible – if that is an option. There is no value to leaving negativity attached to your work, in your blog, or on your social media.

This only applies when you have control over those postings on YouTube or other social media. You can't delete negative comments on Amazon.com and other sites. In those cases, it's best to just leave it alone.

However, it is good idea to read both positive and negative reviews on Amazon, especially in the reviews of your book. As with anything on the Internet, you will run into the occasional harsh criticism for various reasons, but sometimes you'll find a nugget of wisdom. Occasionally, a reader will leave a long review which is useful.

Reviews, good and bad, can help you in various ways. You may decide to revise the current book, which is very easy in the self-publishing world, or you can take the comments to heart for your next book.

The best advice is to ignore criticism and invite critique. Be sure you understand the difference — critique is positive, reinforcing, specific, and actionable, while criticism tends to be general, presented in a negative manner, and disheartening.

Exercise: Write an essay of a page or so about any subject. Ask several people to read it and notice their comments and reactions, then notice your reaction to their comments.

PLAGIARISM

I wrote over three hundred articles for a column that I ran on my website. One day I performed a search and found one of my articles, copied word-for-word, on someone else's website – without my name as the author. In fact, that person claimed he wrote my article.

I sent a nice email, and he chewed me out, saying he loved my article and was only trying to get it out to people who needed the information. I sent him a letter from my lawyer telling him to take it down, which he did immediately.

Chapter 3
Writing

Anything you or anyone else writes is copyrighted from the moment it is created. You do not need to file any special documents or do anything else – the copyright is automatic[4].

This is important to writers and artists because their work has value, and if anyone could take it at will and use it as their own, it would be impossible for creative people to make a living.

Copyright law in the United States allows for something called fair use, which states you can use short quotes from copyrighted works. For example, a movie review can include a few quotes, or even movie clips, from the film, and a book can include quotes from various works from time to time.

However, there is a limit to the amount of material that you can "borrow" from other sources. A few sentences or even a paragraph or two is acceptable, but more than that requires permission.

Outside of fair use, copying from copyrighted material is called plagiarism.

Additionally, if you do use materials from other sources, even if you paraphrase them, you must cite your sources. Include a notation, in one of the standard citation formats, that tells your readers where the information came from. For books, use the

---

[4] This is true for the United States. For other countries, check out the copyright laws that apply.

citation styles described in the Chicago Manual of Style or the Modern Language Style (MLA)[5].

https://style.mla.org/

http://www.chicagomanualofstyle.org/

This is not only good form, but it reinforces your credibility since it shows that you've done your due diligence. It also allows your readers to visit that other source to get more information if desired.

Plagiarism is a serious offense which can lead to legal action – but copyright infringement is not a criminal offense, so you won't go to jail for committing plagiarism (at least not in the USA). However, you can be sued and your reputation could take a hit.

There are several great plagiarism checkers on the Internet; the one I use is PlagScan, because it does a great job at checking sources, and it also creates a nicely formatted Word document complete with citations. This product is not free, but the fees are very reasonable.

https://www.plagscan.com

If you want to learn more about citations, check out the following resource:

http://smooth.li/cite

---

[5] APA (American Psychological Association), the style you probably used in college, is not the appropriate style for books intended for the general public.

**Chapter 3
Writing**

This excellent reference explains all the formatting rules that you should follow when citing other sources and creating your reference page (a list of every source that you've used, usually included as an appendix).

WRITER'S BLOCK

> *I write every day. Most weekdays, I write about ten hours a day. That doesn't mean eight hours of surfing the Net or watching videos on YouTube. I park my butt in a chair and write... I learned that writer's block is a myth created by people who don't have, or understand, a writing process.* – **Jonathan Maberry**

Every writer occasionally suffers from what is commonly known as "writer's block," which is a lack of motivation to write. It can be disconcerting to be moving along at a good clip, writing thousands of words, and suddenly feel like you've run head-on into a wall.

Sometimes it seems that squeezing out a single word is painful and writing an entire paragraph can take hours, or even a whole day. On occasion, writer's block can be so severe that writing ceases for days, weeks, months, or even years at a time.

What causes this debilitating problem?

Sometimes just staring at a computer screen for days on end can drain the motivation from a person. I have found that no matter how motivated I am, writing for hours upon hours at a time inevitably causes my writing to slow to a crawl.

I defeated this problem by scheduling my writing in forty-five minute chunks. By this I mean I literally set a timer for forty-five minutes, and when that buzzer goes off, I stop writing, get out of my chair, and spend the next fifteen minutes doing something else. It's important that this alternative activity does not involve the computer — the idea is to do something other than stare at a computer screen.

Sometimes I take a walk around the block, go for a drive, do an errand, visit a neighbor, or simply do anything else to get my mind off my writing and my eyes away from that hypnotic screen.

As mentioned previously, another common cause of writer's block is hurtful remarks. It's amazing how a simple frown, sarcastic comment, or not-so-subtle lukewarm response can cause so much harm to the writer and the actual writing itself.

For most writers — at least in my experience — writing is a passion and the words we produce are works of art which often come directly from our heart of hearts. Thus, a negative evaluation can cause real harm because it invalidates creativity.

As already stated, criticism is the opposite of critique; criticism is hurtful while critique is helpful. All authors should solicit critique from others because that makes them better writers who will produce better books or materials. On the other hand, no writer should take to heart anything that is said or implied in a critical manner.

For myself, I found this to be a huge source of writer's block. There have been many occasions where I've been zipping along, writing 2,000 to 3,000 words an hour, only to be stopped dead in my tracks by a negative comment from someone else.

Other causes of writer's block include lack of sleep, improper diet, drugs, psychiatric medications, alcohol, and other ethical issues. It's very important for creative people to ensure that they are sleeping right, eating properly, and not imbibing things into their systems that cause the senses to be dulled or altered. Above all, lead a life that makes for a peaceful soul, which in turn will be open and free to writing productively.

Another, and less obvious cause is an emotionally charged environment. A person who is subjected or 'only' exposed to toxicity or abuse, mental or physical, may find their inclination and ability to write diminished.

Highly volatile situations such as going through divorce, conflict at work, the death of a loved one, and other such intense situations or events, can certainly drain the creativity out of a person.

In these cases, I found the best thing to do is to journal my feelings and experiences, and/or to discuss the situation with close friends.

In summary, writer's block is something that every writer faces now and again. Quite often, lack of discipline and poor lifestyle habits are at the cause, and by resolving these, the writer's block can be alleviated.

In other instances, the reasons behind the block are not so obvious, and in this case the best strategy, in my opinion, is to simply persevere and write as much as possible — and separate the writing from the editing.

Chapter 3
Writing

To create a career that makes you a good living as a writer, you must learn to overcome writer's block when it happens. You will experience it, and believe me that it is very disconcerting to feel completely unable to put a single readable sentence down in a manuscript.

Just recognize it for what it is — a temporary block most likely caused by a correctable writing routine, life issue or lifestyle, or dynamic – internal or external – that is affecting or invalidating your writing abilities.

Finally, let me put it this way: if something was preventing you from doing your work at your job, would that be acceptable? Would your boss let you stop working just because you felt like you couldn't, for an extended period, however legitimate the situation was?

If you want to make a living as a self-published author, then treat it like a job or profession. You don't have the luxury of tolerating writer's block. You need to get to the bottom of the problem, get over it, and simply continue writing.

THE GRAMMAR NAZIS

> *Let me just acknowledge that the function of grammar is to make language as efficient and clear and transparent as possible. But if we're all constantly correcting each other's grammar and being really snotty about it, then people stop talking because they start to be petrified that they're going to make some sort of terrible grammatical error and that's precisely the opposite of what grammar is supposed to do, which is to facilitate clear communication.* — **John Green**

At some point in your writing career, you'll run into the Grammar Nazi, who is defined as:

> *A person who habitually corrects or criticizes the language usage of others. – Wiktionary.com*

Some classes and courses teach that your book needs to be free of grammar or spelling errors. While this is certainly true, it can be taken to the extreme and make your life harder than it needs to be.

Your book doesn't need to be perfect. No matter how much you proofread your document, no matter how many times you have it read over by professionals, you will find an occasional grammar and spelling error.

This is just part of the game of being an author.

However, individuals commonly referred to as Grammar Nazis take delight in finding small spelling and grammar errors within your writing.

Chapter 3
Writing

One of my books received a 3-star review that said, "This book was good except for the grammar and spelling errors peppered throughout the manuscript."

When I received that review – my first negative one – I frantically reread the entire manuscript three times, which required several days of effort, to find one spelling error, and two very minor and questionable grammatical errors.

The vast majority of readers happily forgive a few errors in a book. Sometimes, well-meaning and helpful people have sent me an email pointing out specific errors complete with page numbers. I appreciated their efforts, and made the corrections immediately.

To repeat, it doesn't matter how many times you proofread it, or how many times you send it out to professionals, you will have an error or two, or more in your book. Furthermore, editing is as much of an art as it is a science. There is no one perfect version.

Once you've been published, you may receive bad reviews because of those errors. Learn what you can, and don't let them invalidate you or slow you down.

In other words, do the best that you can in the time you have available and move on.

Ensure that your book is a professional quality. After you've written the book, and have gone through it once to make sure that it reads correctly, read it again out loud. Once you've done that, send it off to someone, preferably a professional proofreader, who can catch most of the errors.

In most cases, it's not necessary to do more than that.

Use your time wisely, and focus on what's important.

Your book must be a quality product. But that does not mean it needs to be a perfect product, whatever that means.

You should find a balance between quantity and quality.

CONCLUSIONS

As I've repeated many times so far, to make a living as a self-published author you must simply write. In fact, you must write every single day.

However, ensure you do the research necessary to find the topics that will sell. Otherwise, you'll spend time writing and doing all the other tasks to make your work salable, only to find that your book doesn't break even. That will happen occasionally, even so, but you can reduce the possibility of a poor seller by doing some basic research into your market.

Your books must be of high quality, but being a self-publisher is a business, and if you wish to survive, you need to keep on publishing books. Sometimes a third coat of paint, so to speak, is not necessary.

Proofread your work at least twice all the way through – reading out loud is the best way to find errors. Once you've made it as good as you can, send it to a proofreader or a writing friend and have them review it for errors.

Chapter 3
Writing

If you publish quality books quickly, and promote them well, you may find yourself making money, and that's how you start earning a living as a self-published author.

Chapter 4
Building Your Brand

> *Your author brand (or brands) communicates to your readers*
> *what they can expect from you and gives them reasons to keep*
> *returning for more of your works.*

As your writing career proceeds, it is important to focus on building your brand. A brand is the image that you (or your persona under a pen name) portrays to other people.

Your brand is closely related to your author platform, which is the method used to portray that image. The two are usually discussed as separate specialties, but there is a lot of overlap between the subjects.

One of the most critical components of your brand and your platform is your author blog. Because it's so important, Chapter 6 is entirely devoted to the subject.

Inevitably, you constantly encounter countless brands throughout the day as you watch television, listen to the radio, surf the Internet, read books and magazines, and go about your daily life. A soft drink company might create a brand based on being refreshing and invigorating, while a businessman leading an ethics based company, could want his brand to portray him as a philanthropist involved in high-profile social projects and charities.

Your brand (or brands) is important in that it allows readers to know, like and trust you. The more readers trust you, regardless of whether it's nonfiction or fiction, the more they like you, and the more they feel they know who you are, the more likely they are to purchase your books, write positive reviews, and tell their friends about you.

You may have one main brand, perhaps one for you as an author. Or you may have multiple brands, possibly one for each pen name that you write under. Keep in mind, though, that each brand you create and develop requires that much more effort, which takes away from your daily writing and promotional routine.

You portray your brand in several ways.

- In your author biography in each of your books.
- On your blog via articles, the about page, and photos or drawings.
- What you post on social media.
- During speaking engagements and book signings.
- From interviews on podcasts and radio shows (and if you can swing it, television).

Exercise: Look up four websites of your favorite authors. What brand, if any, do they portray? Are they doing a good or bad job of projecting that image?

YOUR SUBJECTS OR GENRES

Choose your topics to reinforce or define your author brand.

Probably the first decision you'll make when defining your author brand is deciding what you're going to write about.

- Are you going to write fiction, nonfiction, or both?

- Are you going to narrowly focus on one subject or write about many subjects?
- Is your style humorous, casual, formal, or something else?

These and other questions will help define your brand. For instance, Louis L'Amour branded himself as a Western author, while Agatha Christie was known as a writer of mysteries. If you are looking for a science-fiction novel, you would not go looking in the Agatha Christie or Louis L'Amour sections of the bookstore.

These two authors define their brand very narrowly, and because of that, readers know exactly what kind of story they are going to get. This makes them very comfortable with the relative writing style, the storylines, the characters, and the settings. That's one of the reasons why these two authors became well-known and had many bestsellers — readers know what they are going to get, and they know they are going to like what they read.

You can define your brand as anything you want — you can have a narrow focus like Agatha Christie and Louis L'Amour, or you can have a wide focus such as a nonfiction author. You could portray yourself as a security specialist, an expert on writing, or someone knowledgeable and credible in making lots of money.

Spending the time to define and market your brand will go a long way towards increasing your bottom line over the long terms.

Chapter 4
Building Your Brand

Exercise: Sit down, get your paper and pen, and write down a list of subjects you understand and enjoy, or a list of possible topics for fictional stories. Do any of these stand out to you as an area you might want to write several books on?

PEN NAMES

Believe it or not, you can write under any name that you want. In fact, it is quite common for an author to write different topics under different names.

If you have many topics that you want to write about, you can create multiple brands using pen names or pseudonyms. You can write under just about any name you want — although it's bad form to use the name (or a misspelling) of another famous author — and using pen names neatly solves the problem of having a widely-focused brand that may be difficult for you to promote under one identity.

Pen names can also be useful if you want to write about topics that you don't want other people to know you write about. For example, if you are a Western author, you might also write erotic books under a pen name.

Don't expect pen names to prevent people from finding out you wrote certain kinds of books. There is nothing private about pen names, and the more people who are in the know, the more likely it is others will find out. Your publisher, proofreader, cover editor, beta readers, promoters, and others will know your pen name belongs to you.

Pen names are very common in the writing industry, and you shouldn't have any concerns about using them whenever you want. You can use your pen name instead of your real one on the copyright page, the title page, and the book cover, as well as on any promotional materials.

Some so-called authors even go so far as to hire ghostwriters to write books for them which they then publish and sell under pen names.

If you're having trouble fitting the topic of a book into your brand, then a pen name might be just the ticket. Using one can differentiate that topic and, if properly promoted, might improve your sales.

Exercise: Come up with a pen name for a few of the subjects you chose in the last exercise.

Narrow Focus or Wide Net?

> *Do you want to narrowly focus your brand, such as "a writer of Christian books" or a "Security expert"; or perhaps your brand is wider, even as wide as "self-published author". It's completely up to you, depending on the image you want to portray to the world, and how you want to market your books.*

I've made it a point to be a very well educated and well-rounded person. I'm knowledgeable on many subjects, including computers, business, leadership, relationships, even stamps and global warming. This is because I read books constantly, watch documentaries, and attend online and in-person courses on a regular basis.

It's a rare week when I haven't read a book, gone through an online course, reviewed somebody else's book, or watched a documentary. In fact, on most weeks I'll do all the above.

This gives me the advantage of being able to write about a huge variety of subjects, and this is exactly what I have enjoyed doing, as evidenced in my portfolio. I have written books about business, medicine, computers, the Internet of Things, communications, leadership, interpersonal relationships, human rights, interviews I've conducted with interesting people, and apropos to this book and my brand in general – writing related subjects. Heck, I've even published coloring books.

https://www.thewritingking.com/books/

This flies directly in the face of the advice of many promotional and writing experts. Their advice is generally to focus on a single niche and become well-known as the expert in that area. That advice may or may not be useful depending upon your skill level, interests, education, and knowledge.

Indeed, there is a significant value and advantage in being "the expert" on a very narrow subject. This allows you to focus your promotional activities to a well-defined audience. It also makes it easier to build a targeted email list, and your blog will be more focused.

Some authors choose an extremely narrow focus for their niche, even to become so particular as to focus on specific flavors of ice cream, Bible verses, or the history of any one type of doll, such as Barbie.

The disadvantage to a narrow niche is that the taste of readers can change over time, and you may find yourself losing your audience because the niche is no longer popular.

For instance, if your niche is the recent presidential candidate Hillary Clinton, you would probably have found that your audience completely disappeared after she lost the election.

Or if you were an expert at creating Sudoku puzzle books, and you have hundreds of them for sale, you could find your sales dropped as that niche was inundated with new authors trying to make a few quick bucks in a perceived lucrative and profitable area.

Another obvious drawback of this approach is that although one can be creative, each narrow topic can become exhausted even after digging deep.

Chapter 4
Building Your Brand

I've chosen to cast a very wide net on the subjects that I write about. Many authors do this, and as I've already touched upon, it's common to use different pen names or pseudonyms for each subject.

For example, you could write books about cooking under one pen name, then write a book series about military history under another name, and finally produce a series of erotic books under yet a third name.

Regardless of whether you focus on one subject or write about many, once you find that a niche is profitable, it's a good idea to focus a lot of energy in that area. Even though I write about many different subjects, once I discovered that money-making books are profitable, I devoted much of my promotional energy towards that niche.

How do you find a niche? Look for areas where your passion and other people's passions intersect. I'm passionate about writing and publishing. And with some research, as described in Chapter 2, I determined that others are attempting to make a living in this area but are lacking real-world guidance, and thus they are passionate about the subject as well.

Because those passions intersect, I channeled my natural talents, skills, education, experience, and knowledge into that area, and it's likely others will be interested as well and will purchase my books.

It's much easier to find a niche that is already developed than it is to create a new one. In fact, unless you're very lucky, it's virtually impossible to develop a new niche, especially for a beginning author.

A good exercise is to find yourself an inspiring and private corner somewhere, and write out all the various subjects where you have education, skills, interest, or passion.

Once you have that list, head over to Amazon and check out the books in those areas. Look at the books on the first page of a search by that subject and see how well they're selling. You can do this by going to a book page and scrolling down to a section titled "Product Details". In that section, you'll find in bold, "Amazon Best Sellers Rank".

If that number is very high, say over a million, that book is not selling very well. On the other hand, if the value is low, in the order of 5000 to 10,000, the book is making good sales. The higher the number, the worse the book is selling, and the lower the number, the better it is selling.

Check out a dozen books in that niche, and you'll soon get a feel for how well those books are doing. Perform this exercise for every item on your list until you find a niche that works for you. If nothing on your list is selling well, then you may have to widen your horizons and add a few more subjects until you find one that works.

This method is not foolproof by any means. Following this advice, I determined that LinkedIn was a very lucrative niche. Unfortunately, it turned out that people were not interested in spending money to develop their LinkedIn profile. I could give away thousands of copies, sell thousands of them at ninety-nine cents, but once I raised the price to something reasonable, like $4.99, my sales dried up.

Chapter 4
Building Your Brand

There are other methods you can use to help you reinforce your conclusion that a niche is lucrative before you spend the time writing a book. You can survey people on Facebook or other social media, or in writing or other groups; you can grab a clipboard and walk around the neighborhood and talk to people; or you can even have conversations with patrons at bookstores to find out what they're interested in.

The point is that you want to spend some upfront time determining if a niche will work before you take the effort to write a book.

Remain flexible, and write and publish books quickly. That way, if you find that a niche is not making sufficient income, you can move on to a different one without having expended a dramatic amount of effort and wasted lots of time.

Exercise: Pick a category on Amazon and select a book. Look at the book detail page, and scroll until you find the book details section. Look at the "Amazon Best Sellers Rank". How well is it doing? Try this for several books in different categories.

Next, get your notebook and visit your local bookstore. Look at what is on the shelves, and have a conversation with one of the store employees. See if you can come to an informed conclusion about what is selling well.

QUALITY OR QUANTITY?

What's more important to a self-published author – publishing a lot of books efficiently, or spending the time to make each one perfect?

The other day I was reading an article that said you should begin prepping your social media to expect your book publication at least four, and preferably eight, months before the launch date.

That strategy is useful for a major book, one that you plan to spend a lot of time writing and promoting. However, for books that you write and publish quickly, in a matter of days, you won't to be able to do this.

The concept of a book launch comes from the world of traditional publishing, where it often takes a year or more from when a book is submitted to a publisher until it finally appears on the bookshelves at bookstores.

In my case, I have a few books that are important to my "core" brand. These build my credibility and showcase my knowledge, skills and talents, and tend to be 30,000 or more words long.

My strategy is to write a longer book of this nature every few months, then spend the time to do a formal book launch and more significant promotion. In between those longer works, I quickly and efficiently write and publish shorter, straight-to-the point books.

The truth of the matter is that the more books you have for sale – in other words the more titles you have out there – the more money you're going to make. Of course, there's always that odd exception of a book that shoots to the top of the charts either on its own, or after a big promotion.

Speed is an important and vital corollary. The faster you get those books written, proofread, beta read, edited, published, and promoted, the faster you start making money. Conversely, the longer you take between books, the less money you make.

This doesn't imply that you should be pumping out poor-quality books. Not by any means. The point is you need to streamline your process so that you get your books from idea to publication and promotion quickly.

Why is this true?

The simple fact of the matter is that books remain in Amazon's database (or the database of wherever you published it) available to be purchased, from the moment you publish them for as long as you keep them listed. Thus, each book in your portfolio can potentially get sales every day, every week, and every month for the rest of your life.

If you are doing some basic promotion for each book – Amazon Marketing Services is ideal for this purpose – then you'll potentially continue to make anywhere from a few dollars to a few hundred dollars each month from every book that you have published. Of course, it is true that some books will not sell at all during a single month; however, others may sell hundreds of copies.

The key points to remember are:

- Publish as many books as you can, as fast as you can.
- Ensure those books are of high quality.
- Ensure your promotional materials – which include the book cover, description, title, book reviews, and so on – are up to snuff.
- Use Amazon Marketing Services and other promotional methods to drive traffic to your books.

The reason why I keep bringing up Amazon Marketing Services is that once you have it set up and have done a little fine-tuning until it produces traffic, then you can pretty much forget about it. This makes it ideal for supporting a portfolio of many books.

I wrote a product which describes in detail how to use AMS. You can find it here:

> http://smooth.li/amsatm
> *Note, this is an affiliate link. If you purchase the product I will receive a small commission.*

Of course, it's much easier to focus on one book than it is to focus on many. As a result, any way you can automate the process, especially promotion-wise, will be helpful in improving your profits and reducing your efforts.

Think of a book as a product that you're selling to an audience. Your book may sell very well or, what's most likely, you'll sell a few dozen copies, especially if you don't promote it properly.

Chapter 4
Building Your Brand

If you have only one book to sell, regardless of how well it does, you're only going to profit from that one product. It may sell great for a short period (unless you're lucky or have a lot of money to spend on promotion) but eventually sales will sag and the money will stop coming in.

On the other hand, if you have a large quantity of books, spikes and valleys amongst titles or categories will balance themselves out to help you maintain a steadier flow of income.

How much time should you spend on each book?

Spend as much time as you need to have a book of reasonable quality that delivers your message the way you desire. My production goal is to take an 8,000 to 12,000-word book from idea to published product in three to five days.

At that speed, I can publish from one to three books of that size every week. That's if I'm working on writing books steadily without any interruptions such as freelance writing assignments (for pay), vacations, or anything else.

My minimum goal is to publish one book per week. That gives me time for paid freelance writing gigs, promoting specific books, writing products, putting together courses, and other things.

Speed of publication, or in other words, the quantity of books you desire to write and publish, is a decision that you'll have to make. A lot of it depends on how much time you have available to write, whether you're writing is a career or just a hobby, and the amount of knowledge and experience you possess regarding your niche or subjects.

FONTS, STYLES AND COLORS

> *The individual components of your branding should reinforce one another.*

The colors, styles and fonts that you choose for your blog, promotional materials, advertising, business card, and everything else say something to your readers.

Purple has meant royalty for millennia, red tends to mean danger or energy, while green or brown may suggest the outdoors.

I recently published a book, *Network Your Business to Profit*, and originally created a red cover. Upon consulting with a design expert, she told me that red means anger or emotion, which is great for a self-help book. However, for business a calmer color such as blue would be better for my audience. I took her advice.

The most important characteristic when you pick a font is that it be readable. This is especially true on the cover of a book, where the first view by a reader is of a thumbnail.

Some fonts portray sincerity or romance, some envision child-like fantasy, while others suggest stylishness.

Additionally, the styles that you use within your blog pages and elsewhere can communicate a lot more than you might think. Blocky images may portray a more structured or practical style, while circular images could suggest more creativity or fluidity.

Chapter 4
Building Your Brand

Even the positioning of images and fonts can make a difference in the appeal of a book cover. A sloppy cover with titles that are not properly centered, fonts that don't line up, and images that are seemingly randomly placed will look amateurish, and that's definitely NOT going to lead to better sales.

Professional designers deal with decisions about which fonts, styles and colors to use all the time. Choosing the right combination is an important decision for your brand, and it's best to get the advice of someone who has been trained in the area before committing to anything.

This doesn't mean you shouldn't go ahead and create your blog, business cards, and do the necessary promotion. My own materials went through several iterations before I finally met with an artistic designer who helped me create the brand that portrays an image that feels exactly right. The Writing King symbolizes the qualities of royalty, such as self-assuredness and influence, so it was important to me that the colors, fonts, and styles generated that mental picture.

Exercise: Surf to several different websites and note how the different fonts, colors, and styles work together – or how they don't.

Logo

One of the most important elements of your brand is your logo. Your logo should be simple with only a few colors (and it should look good in black-and-white as well) so it is easily recognized and memorable.

Display your logo on your business cards, website or blog, stationery, invoices, on your book cover pages, and just about everywhere else that may be seen by your customers or readers.

It's important that the logo portray whatever characteristics are central to your brand in an obvious and meaningful way.

Don't choose a logo from a stock logo or image site, and don't use sites such as Fiverr.com for this purpose. Instead, engage the services of a professional logo designer if possible. This is a specialty which requires a certain degree of artistic talent along with specialized training. I was amazed, after trying with four or five different people, at the level of quality I got from a real professional.

For example, I engaged the services of a local company, *Laura's Design Studio*, and she created my logo and helped design my website. Meeting with someone in person to design a logo or a website is an entirely different, and much more fulfilling, experience than trying to work with them over the web.

http://laurasdesignstudio.com/

The value of meeting with someone in person to communicate your requirements, talk about revisions, and build a

103

relationship so that they truly understand what you want is, in my opinion, something that cannot easily be done over the web.

Building a relationship is key. Your designer will ensure you get the correct file types for print and web. Once you have your logo you can build off it and begin to create your brand.

You can expect to pay a minimum of $200 for a simple logo by a professional graphics designer, and the price can go up to $500 or even $1,000 for more complex designs.

If you can't afford to pay a graphics designer directly, explore the idea of trading services. For example, you could trade writing copy on their website or a few blog articles for a good logo design.

Make sure you get all the source files for the logo so you're not stuck with working with the same designer.

Your logo files should be delivered in vector graphics so that it can be resized without losing any details. Additionally, get a black and white version for promotion that is not printed in color.

Exercise: Look at the logos of several major companies (from their web sites) such as LinkedIn, eBay, Coca-Cola, and so on. Note how the logo delivers a message reinforcing the corporate branding.

AUTHOR BIO

Readers want to know about you, the author. How did you learn to write? What events in your life led to you writing your books or a book?

Many writers overlook or downgrade the importance of an author biography. That's unfortunate, because a good bio section can improve the relationship with your readers, gives information to the media, and helps improve your brand and reputation.

Remember, you will improve your sales by getting your readers to know, like and trust you; this concept is explained fully in my book *Network Your Business to Profit*. A biography helps to address the "know" portion of this formula.

A well-written bio targeted to the brand that you are trying to portray helps readers make up their minds, not just to buy your book, but to follow you and see what other books, and possibly products you have for sale.

This is especially true when working with the media. If you're going to do public speaking, book signings, or give interviews for podcasts, radio, and television, having an author bio provides information about you in an easily accessible place.

You want to make your bio interesting, engaging, and directed wholly towards your brand. In other words, you want to answer the question "what makes you the expert about this book (or books or book series) you have written?"

Chapter 4
Building Your Brand

Author biographies are generally written in the third person, as if someone was telling your readers about you, although first-person can work on occasion.

Your job in writing your bio is to tell readers why you are an authority on the subject in your book. What makes you an authority and why should anyone care about what you have written?

Include information such as:

- Awards that you have won.
- Books you have written.
- Speeches you have given.
- Articles you've published.
- Articles and other materials published about you.
- Podcasts you've appeared in.
- Interviews you've received.
- Any other honors that you have received that reinforce your credibility.
- Exclude anything that has little or nothing to do with your brand.

Don't worry if you don't get it right the first time. Your author biography, especially the one on your blog or website, should be an organic document that changes over time. After all, you will ideally be publishing more books, receiving more honors and awards, making more speeches, and so forth.

Where does your bio appear?

- On the About page of your website. This should be the longest and most complete version.
- In the back of each of your books.
- In the biography section of Amazon Author Central.
- On your LinkedIn, Facebook, and other social media profiles.
- On your Facebook pages.
- On various association websites.
- In your Meetup.com profile.
- As part of your media kit.
- Anywhere else that asks for a biography or profile.

These profiles do not (and should not) be identical, but they should all provide a consistent story about you and your brand.

How important is the author biography? Many times, a good bio is what sells your book to readers, bookstores, and libraries. Put yourself in the shoes of a librarian who has a limited budget. Before stocking your book on their shelves, they want to know if you're the right person to deliver your topic to their readers.

Your bio is a vital part of your branding and promotional strategy. Spend the time to get it right, and be willing to have multiple variations for different purposes. Additionally, rewrite it as often as you need to as time goes by.

Chapter 4
Building Your Brand

Exercise: Set aside a few hours to write your author biography for your blog. Put it aside for a day, then review it and make any corrections you need.

AUTHOR VIDEO

An author video, which is essentially a marketing tool, can build interest for your readers. As a rule, people love watching videos, and it is certainly the best way to communicate a large amount of information quickly.

Some people love video and some hate it. Personally, I fall into the latter category as I'm not very fond of videos of myself. However, there are others who thrive on regular video podcasts or YouTube channels — these people are usually extroverts or have learned to work around their introverted tendencies.

However, an author video, which can be like an author bio in video form, can be a very powerful way to express your brand. After all, the video is the author talking about themselves in their own words.

There are different kinds of author videos possible:

- **Explainer video** — Usually animated and explains something in picture and word form. These are generally easy to put together and don't require the author being on camera.

- **Interview video** — A videotaped interview of the author, either made specifically for the purpose, or taken from a media source.
- **Marketing video** — These are created specifically to market an author, generally by a professional service.
- **Podcast video** — If so inclined, an author can put out a regular video series and use the most recent one as their author video.

There are undoubtedly many other kinds of videos that you can create to describe yourself as an author to your readers.

If you decide to create an author video, you can hire a professional service, preferably local to you, to design, shoot, and edit it for you. Creating this kind of video can be complicated, and such specialties such as lighting, makeup, and body position can mean the difference between a mediocre and an excellent video.

Alternately, you can make a video yourself using your smartphone, computer webcam or other device, and edit it using video editing software. These types of homemade videos can be powerful since they are of an author speaking directly to their readers in a natural and real way. If you are going to video yourself, using a tripod (for a digital camera) or a selfie-stick (for a phone) to make it easier.

Exercise: Use your smartphone camera or the webcam on your computer to create a quick, 1 to 3 minute video of you talking about your background.

Chapter 4
Building Your Brand

Author Photo or Image

> *Spend the time and money to get professional photos taken for you to use on your blog, provide to the media and for profiles of all your social media accounts.*

One of the most important components of your branding package is your author photo. Readers want to physically see their favorite authors because it helps them feel a connection with the writer, and if the photo has the right elements, it will inspire likability and trust.

In most cases, your author photo should be an actual photograph, although in the case of coloring and comic books, an avatar (an image of the author) can be used instead. If you're writing under a pseudonym, and you don't wish to be known under that name, you can use a drawing of a fictional author instead of a photo.

If you use a photograph, hire a professional photographer. This is one area of your branding where the money is well spent, and a poor photograph will detract immensely from your credibility.

Some of the types of photographs that you should avoid include:

- **Selfies** — Don't use selfies at all, unless you're writing a book about selfies.
- **Personal photos that are cropped** — Cropped photos just look tacky and amateurish.
- **Photos taken by your friend or associate** — Unless your friend is a professional photographer, you're

almost certainly going to wind up with a substandard picture.

- **Outdated photos** — Use a recent photo, not something from high school or college. If you're fifty years old, a photograph of you when you were twenty-two is not appropriate.
- **Photos with other people in the picture** — There are instances where this can be appropriate, such as in the case of a book about your genealogy or family history, but otherwise you should be the only person in the photo.

Instead, your photograph should have the following characteristics:

- **Professional headshot** — A professional headshot, perhaps in black-and-white, works very well.
- **Good lighting** — One of the reasons to use a professional photographer is that they will ensure the lighting is appropriate and makes you look good.
- **Lack of distractions in the background** — The photograph should focus on you and not on the beer bottles, messy kitchen, or pool table in the background.
- **Smiling** — As a rule, people like to see smiles, so it's important to smile in your photo. A sincere, happy smile gives you an approachable and friendly appearance.
- **Well-groomed and well dressed** — Make sure you look good for your photo, with a nice haircut or styling and good, clean clothes.

Chapter 4
Building Your Brand

- **Match your brand** — If you write Westerns then you might consider wearing western attire. Don't take this too far, but a few subtle touches may add to your brand. For example, if you write Star Trek fan-fiction, then you might wear a Star Trek pen on your lapel.

Your author photo should appear in your biography and media packet, and on your social media. Make sure your photos match across all your media.

Finally, ensure that you replace your headshot at least every couple of years, if not more often. Your picture should reflect the way you look now, not how you looked years ago. Besides, a change can attract some good attention.

MEDIA PACKET

> *Make it easy for members of the press to get information about you by providing a media packet on your blog.*

A media packet is a page on your blog containing everything needed for someone in the media to use to write stories in their publications about you.

The media includes television, radio, podcasters, bloggers, newspapers, and other channels used to talk to the public. As you become more popular, and send out press releases and so forth, you're going to get requests for information about you, your book series, your books, and so forth, so it's best to have it already prepared so you don't have to do the work over and over.

I found it's best to create a PDF containing everything in one easy place to make it easy to print out. Don't secure this document as you want anyone to be able to copy and paste from your kit as needed.

Include some or all of the following:

- Introduce yourself and your business.
- Describe your mission – what are you trying to do?
- Include a few testimonials.
- Answer any frequently asked questions.
- List your book series and books.
- Describe any supporting statistics – book sales, bestseller status and so forth.
- Of course, include your primary contact information.

Spend the time to make this document practical, descriptive, and compelling to members of the media. Everything should reflect a positive image of you and your brand.

AMAZON BOOK PAGE

For every book that you publish, Amazon creates a page which includes all the information about it. This showcases your book and is designed to entice people to get the information they need to make a purchase.

The book page consists of one page for each version of your book. Thus, you'll have a page for your Kindle version, paperback, hardcover, and audiobook. Each one of these pages can contain subtly or markedly different information.

Chapter 4
Building Your Brand

For example, you can have a different description for your paperback than you do for your hardcover version.

- The front and back covers of your book.
- The "look inside" feature, which allows people to see the first 10% or so of your book before they purchase. It's important to know that this does not appear right away after you publish – it can take as long as three or four weeks.
- The title, subtitle, and book series.
- The date the book was published. This date does not change if you update the contents of your book.
- The description of your book.
- All the reviews of all your versions are merged together on all pages. Thus, you'll see Kindle, paperback, and audiobook reviews, for example, merged together on the page for each format.
- A small block containing information about your book such as the number of pages, its ranking, the publisher, and its ranking within each category defined for your book.
- The ASIN or ISBN number of your book. If you specify an ISBN number for your Kindle volume, it will not be listed. Instead, the ASIN is always listed for that format.
- You'll also find advertising for other, similar books, including your own if they apply. This advertising[6] is different for every single person on Amazon, and changes depending upon what they viewed, purchased, and have inside of their wish lists.

---

[6] These advertisements are purchased from many sources, including Amazon Marketing Services, which is available to self-published authors.

- You can include a video trailer for your book on that page and on the Author's page you can add your blog, so there is always new content on there, which allows you to add new trailers to promote all of your newest books.

It's important to understand that you have control over most of the information on these pages. You specify the title, subtitle, series, description and publishing company, among other things. For more information, see chapter 10, Metadata.

Most of this information can be changed after you publish the book. For Kindle books, virtually everything can be changed at any time. On paperbacks and hardcovers, the title, subtitle, author, ISBN number, publishing company and series cannot be changed once you've published the book. You can change the information on audiobooks, but you'll have to re-record and resubmit the opening and closing segments if you change the title.

All the versions of a book usually link together on the same book page automatically. If, after a couple of days, this doesn't happen, you can use the "contact" field in your KDP or CreateSpace dashboard to ask their support group to do it for you. They are always very happy to help and very competent (send them the ASIN or ISBN for the books you want to link together).

Exercise: Examine several book pages on Amazon and get familiar with all the various parts and sections.

THE BOOK PAGE URL

Each book page is given a unique link (URL) which you can use in your advertising, promotions, and anywhere else to reference your book. The link for any version may be used, since all versions work together on the same page.

> https://www.amazon.com/
> Real-World-Survival-Preparing-
> Surviving/dp/1943517037/ref=asap_bc?ie=UTF8

Above is shown a sample raw link to one of my book pages. The number "1943517037" is the ISBN number of that book.

When you use that link anywhere else, remove the "/ref" and everything following as it is unnecessary. Thus, the link above becomes:

> https://www.amazon.com/
> Real-World-Survival-Preparing-
> Surviving/dp/1943517037/

If you have an Amazon affiliate account, then in your promotions and on your blog, include "?tag=affiliate" where "affiliate" is your Amazon affiliate identifier. Thus, the link above using my affiliate ID would become:

> https://www.amazon.com/
> Real-World-Survival-Preparing-
> Surviving/dp/1943517037/?tag=thewritingkin-20

MYBOOK.TO AND SMARTURL.IT

You can use a service called MyBook.To to provide links to your books.

> http://MyBook.To

Simply go to that site and enter the Amazon link to your book. Once you've done that, you'll be asked for a short name which is used to identify the book.

Thus, the link for my book *Real World Survival*:

> https://www.amazon.com/Real-World-Survival-Tips-Guide-ebook/dp/B011AI5YUG

Becomes:

> http://myBook.to/Disaster

Be sure to trim the book link as described in the previous section (The Book Page URL).

Not only is this easier to remember, MyBook.To also collects statistics on the number of times this link is clicked. This can be very valuable to determine if your promotion is working.

Use the service SmartUrl.It to create similar links that send your readers to different Amazon sites depending upon what country they are in. This is useful if you have Amazon Affiliate codes for the different countries supported by Amazon.

> http://smarturl.it

Chapter 4
Building Your Brand

It's a lot of work to set up SmartUrl.It, and unless your book sells well in other countries (and you have an affiliate account for Amazon in those locations) then it's probably not worth the trouble.

AUTHOR CENTRAL

After you publish your first book, head on over to Amazon Author Central at the following link:

https://authorcentral.amazon.com/

This is a wonderful set of tools that Amazon has provided to help you promote your books. You can add more information to your book pages, create an author bio, add multimedia such as video, and so forth.

Part of your routine for each book should be to ensure that as many fields as appropriate are filled in. This information will appear on your book pages and help convince readers to purchase your books.

Be sure to link your blog to your author central account. By doing this, every post you make on your blog will also be made on Amazon.

Exercise: Proceed to Author Central and create an account. Look over the options.

AMAZON MARKETING SERVICES

One of the very first things that you should do once your book is published and live on Amazon is get into Amazon Marketing Services (AMS) and create one or more advertisements. AMS is a pay per click service which allows authors to purchase advertising for their books on Amazon.

To advertise on AMS, your book needs to be in Kindle format published through KDP. However, since other versions, such as hardcover and paperback are on the same book page, people will be able to buy them as well.

To keep the explanation simple, create a sponsored advertisement, choose one of your books, write a short ad, then list keywords and phrases to go with the book.

Define the maximum amount that can be spent each day for each ad, and the maximum bid for each keyword.

AMS is simple – don't overcomplicate it. You don't need to spend a lot of time researching keywords and overthinking the whole process. Put in as many keywords as you can that might apply to your book, as many as a hundred, 200, 300 or more. Amazon will automatically favor those that apply, and those that don't won't get impressions.

You are only charged for clicks and not impressions, and then only up to your budget amount. Initially, keep the budget small, I like to start at $1 a day per ad, and raise it as you see that the advertisement is working for you.

If an advertisement is costing less than 50% of what you are making, then it is working and you can give it a bigger budget.

Chapter 4
Building Your Brand

If you're spending more than 50% of your profits, aggressively look through the keywords and phrases and pause those that are costing too much for the amount you made.

This entire process is described fully in a product that I wrote called AMS ATM. You can get your copy at the following link:

> http://smooth.li/amsatm
> *Note, this is an affiliate link. If you purchase the product I will receive a small commission.*

AMS is an excellent tool and you should take advantage of it to promote your books. It's simple, easy-to-use and, after some tuning, works on autopilot. This means you'll make money without doing more than adjusting a few parameters now and then.

Exercise: Create an Amazon Marketing Services account. Once you are inside, examine the help files and options.

CONCLUSIONS

Your brand is what helps set you apart from other authors and gives your readers a sense of who you are and why you are credible. Make sure you spend the time and money to build the appropriate image for your niche and personality.

Consistency is the key to creating a good, strong brand that attracts readers and causes them to want to purchase your books. They need to know you (via the author biography and media packet), like you (regular communications) and trust you (deliver quality books).

Most importantly – if you don't take the time to create an author brand, your readers and others will create one for you, without your directed guidance or input. Is that what you really want?

Chapter 5
Author Platform

> *Audience development doesn't happen overnight (or even in 6 months or a year)—and it's a process that continues for as long as you want to have a readership. It shouldn't be delayed, postponed, or discounted for one minute.* – ***Jane Friedman***

Your author platform is the stage on which you present your books and your brand to your public. Creating and maintaining a platform is vital to making your books sell and to gaining the interest of booksellers, libraries, and traditional publishers.

How you reach your public depends upon your personality, skills, likes and dislikes. Some authors prefer video, others create audio podcast channels, and others simply blog several times a week.

Regardless of the platform or media you choose, it needs to succeed at attracting and engaging readers. A platform requires a lot of effort, and it's wasted time if it doesn't help build your credibility, increase your sales, and improve engagement.

Think about stretching your boundaries a bit. If you're introverted, try getting interviewed for podcasts or give a speech at your local library. You might be surprised to find that you enjoy those activities.

Regardless of whatever platform you choose, host the materials on your own blog. This gives you a home base for people to find everything about you and your books.

Chapter 5
Author Platform

EMAIL LIST

> *If you don't have an email list, you're throwing away money.*

We'll get into Email Lists more thoroughly in Chapter 7.

One of the most important tasks at the top of your to-dos is to create and build an email list. This is your primary method for staying in contact with your readers. Using your list, you can occasionally send out updates about your works in progress, new books you've published, and any other information you believe your readers will find valuable.

To begin, choose an email list provider. A good one for those who are starting out is MailChimp, as the entry level is free, and stays affordable as your list grows. MailChimp is full-featured, and has automation that makes sending messages to your subscribers simple and straightforward.

http://mailchimp.com

Your email list should include several autoresponder letters. These are messages that are timed a certain number of days apart, which are automatically sent out to your subscribers. For example, you'll probably send out a welcome message as soon as somebody subscribes, then you might send a biography of yourself three days later, followed by a list of your books three days after that, followed by some information about a product you're selling.

You can include as many letters in an autoresponder sequence as you want. This is a way to set up communications to your readers without having to do the work repeatedly. Be careful to ensure that the messages you send out are 'evergreen', meaning they're not dated.

Additionally, you can send out letters on demand to your list for new books and promotions.

Get people to join your list by offering them a free product of some sort – a downloadable PDF, a video, or something of value, in exchange for them providing their name and email address.

Set up your email list at the same time you set up your blog – the two go together as methods to communicate with your readers. Regardless of whatever other methods you use in your author platform, an email list and a blog are essential.

Exercise: Create an account at MailChimp.com and go through their help files and tutorials to get an idea of how it works. Does this help you understand how this can help your promotions?

BOOK SIGNINGS

> *In my own book-signings, I find humility. It's always humbling when people go out of their way to come visit with me and buy some of my books.* — **Nicholas Trandahl**

One of the reasons to make your book available in paperback and hardcover is so that you can order copies for yourself to use and sell at book signings.

Chapter 5
Author Platform

These events are put on by bookstores, writing associations, local business groups, libraries, and even authors themselves to attract the public and build up buzz about their book. They can last anywhere from thirty minutes to all day, and can include one or more authors.

Both the author and the venue have a responsibility to invite people to the signing. Ensure you send invitations to local news sources, your email list, any of your groups, Facebook, and so on. Consider sending out a press release with an announcement to get even more people to attend.

A book tour consisting of multiple book signings in different areas of the city, state, or even country, can do wonders to promote your works. I know from personal experience there's nothing like meeting an author in person, even for just a minute or two, to get their personal note and signature on a copy of their book.

I remember meeting Kelly Reno at the World Mermaid Awards show in Las Vegas in 2011 (I photographed the event). She had a stack of her books on a table and signed a copy of Misadventures & Merfolk, her most recent novel, with a personal message.

http://smooth.li/mermaids

Other personally signed books include *Beneath Lies Beauty* by Jacqueline Collen-Tarrolly (a good friend, beautiful model, and actress who played Mauve in the show *Adventures of Sinbad* which ran from 1996 to 1998) and *Showgirl Confidential* by Pleasant Gehman, another great friend and a famous burlesque and belly dancer. Getting signed copies from these authors was a wonderful experience and ensured I'd be on the lookout for their future works.

The point is to create a memorable experience for those who arrive. Be well-dressed, on your best behavior, shake everyone's hand and sell signed copies of your books. Spend the time to talk to everyone and listen, and don't forget to take a few pictures (or even short videos) of you with your fans at these events. These videos and pictures are great for your blog and social media.

You can begin your book signing adventures at your local library. They won't pay you for your time but you will be selling your books to make a few extra dollars.

Your marketing should plan book signings as a regular part of your itinerary for promotion, even if those events are just in your local area. This will help build up buzz in the community about you and your works.

Exercise: Use your favorite search engine to find your local library. Send them an email asking for information about how to set up a book signing.

PUBLIC SPEAKING

> *If you have an important point to make, don't try to be subtle or clever. Use a pile driver. Hit the point once. Then come back and hit it again. Then hit it a third time - a tremendous whack.* — **Winston S. Churchill**

Jumping into public speaking is one of the most difficult barriers for many authors, yet it is one of the best ways to get your name out there. You can speak at your local Chamber of Commerce, networking meetings, businesses, libraries, special events, conventions, and anywhere else.

To break the ice and learn how to speak in public join a local Toastmasters group. This organization is dedicated to helping people prepare and present speeches, and the cost is low. I'm a member myself, and I recommend that all authors join their local group and attend the meetings regularly.

http://www.toastmasters.org/

Record all your speaking events (including those done at Toastmasters meetings) in both audio and video formats, and have someone take pictures. After your speech, send the audio recording to a transcriber. This allows you to use the whole speech, or selected parts, in your promotional materials. Edit the transcription carefully — it's okay to change it is much as you want — to correct any errors and make it more appropriate for your purposes.

The video and pictures can be used for your book trailers, promotional materials, on your blog, and can even be sent to members of the press. You can also edit videos as desired to use specific portions to suit your needs.

If you do record – either in audio, video or both – your speaking engagements, edit and file them as you go. Otherwise, you'll find yourself with a large backlog of material that is difficult or impossible to search.

Taking the plunge to speak in public about your subject is a wonderful way to improve your credibility and your confidence. You may even find, as I did, much to my surprise, that you enjoy speaking to groups.

Exercise: Visit Toastmasters.Org and find a local Toastmasters near you with a meeting time that you can attend, then visit it as a guest, which is free.

RADIO SHOWS AND PODCASTS

> *"Your comfort zone is a place where you keep yourself in a self-illusion and nothing can grow there but your potentiality can grow only when you can think and grow out of that zone."* – **Rashedur Ryan Rahman**

Another excellent way to gain exposure is to get featured on radio shows and Internet podcasts. This is relatively easy to do. Use your search engine to find podcasts and radio shows, send them a quick email, and offer them your expertise in the form of a guest appearance.

There are thousands (probably tens of thousands) of podcasts all over the web, and most of them need guests to fill up their airtime. If you can speak intelligently and answer questions about your book or specialties, then you could easily do several interviews a week.

If you want to make the process go faster, you can get a premium membership on Radioguestlist.com, which is a site that helps podcast and radio shows find guests.

http://www.radioguestlist.com

Purchasing a premium subscription gets you your own page listed with information about yourself and what you offer to hosts.

Exercise: Visit Radioguestlist.com and get on their email list. Several times a week you'll receive a list of hosts that need guests. Either send an email, or call these hosts until you get one that agrees to an interview.

SOCIAL MEDIA

> *Social media is the ultimate equalizer. It gives a voice and a platform to anyone willing to engage.* — **Amy Jo Martin**

Social media is an essential way for all authors to engage their fans and readers. If you are not active on social media, posting several times a day on different platforms, then you are missing out on one of the best methods to connect with your audience.

Social media is not intended for advertising or promotion. Sites such as Facebook, Google Plus, LinkedIn, and

Goodreads were created to facilitate social interaction between people, not pimp products and services. Obvious advertising and promotion tends to be frowned upon or completely ignored. Continuous promotion will cause your readers to tune out and ignore you and your message.

You want to make social media work for you? Interact socially with the people on the various platforms. When you post "buy my book" or "join my Kickstarter", you are not talking to people – you are throwing mud at the walls to see what sticks. It doesn't work.

Post materials that reinforce your credibility and build a relationship with readers.

Some of the things you can do that will help, include:

- Post questions related to your niche.
- Post links to articles on blogs other than your own.
- Post links to articles on your own blog (note that some groups consider this self-promotion).
- Write short, one or two paragraph articles related to your specialty.
- If visual aids help reinforce your brand or niche, post graphics or images.
- Answer other people's questions, even if they are not related to your niche.
- Treat people with respect, and talk to them as people, not as credit cards or cash machines.

People are not active on social media to buy your books. They are there to socialize, to talk to people, to discuss things and

to play games. Get involved, educate, entertain, and you'll find over time you'll gain followers who will buy your books.

This is because they start to know, like and trust you. That's the whole point of interacting on social media as an author. Get your audience to know who you are, like you, and trust you. If you can do that, you'll sell books.

Exercise: Write a couple of paragraphs about a subject that is of interest to readers of your book, whether or not it is of interest to you. Post this to your social media.

DAILY QUOTES

> *For the great majority of you, cut down on the number of inspirational quotes you post. An entire generation will thank you.*
> — **Anqi Cong**

Some authors (and others trying to sell things) have gotten the idea that posting graphics with funny, wise, or spiritual sayings on them is a way to get engagement and attract readers.

You might, for example, post a word of inspiration, along with the URL of your web site, on a graphic every day of the week. The idea is to keep your brand (the URL) in front of people all the time.

This may have worked in the past, but the technique has been so overused that these are largely ignored.

Focus your promotional methods on engaging with your readers by communicating with them as human beings and you'll have more success.

FACEBOOK

> *Facebook was not originally created to be a company. It was built to accomplish a social mission - to make the world more open and connected.* — **Mark Zuckerberg**

Second only to YouTube, Facebook is the most important social media platform for interacting with your readers. Create Facebook pages and groups for this interaction. Don't use your personal Facebook account – don't make or accept friend requests from your readers – instead, ask them to like your pages and join your groups.

It's important to maintain the separation between your personal life, represented by your personal Facebook profile, and your business life, represented by your Facebook pages and groups.

If you've already got readers who are friends with you on Facebook, don't worry about it. But going forward, use pages and groups instead.

Otherwise, you may find that personal information, photos, and schedules get leaked to inappropriate people and the press outside of your control. In some instances, inviting non-friends into your personal social media results in physical stalking and worse.

Chapter 5
Author Platform

Create a Facebook page for each of your significant books or series as well as one for you as an author. The process isn't difficult and it is free of charge. Use these pages to increase engagement and give readers consistent places where they can find out about you (your general-purpose author page) and your major works (each book page).

For example, I've created a Facebook page called "Richard Lowe author", plus one for my books *Focus on LinkedIn*, *How to Sell on eBay*, *Real World Survival*, and for my line of coloring books: *The Coloring King*. Each page took me about an hour to create, which included a few minutes to find a graphic on Pixabay.com (a free image site). I used book covers as logos for each of the book-related pages, my photograph for *Richard Lowe Author*, and a coloring book logo for The Coloring King page.

Each day, I spend half an hour in the morning and half an hour in the evening posting to those pages. Typically, I'll post a video to one page, a couple of paragraph status updates to all the pages (each one different), create an event for a book signing, create a poll on another one, and answer a few questions from readers.

Create a separate page for each significant book or book series that you are promoting, but don't go overboard and create more pages than you can conveniently work on in a 30-minute timeframe.

The idea is that you have different audiences for different books or series, so you can build a more focused following by creating different pages for each. This makes your conversations and communications more relevant to their interests.

My main page, *Richard Lowe Author*, ties everything together, and to it I post information about other books, scheduled events, general articles, and other relevant information.

If you don't have blog, then a Facebook Page can serve as a free and simple substitute. You can't do as much with it as you can with a blog, and you don't have as much control, but it's better than nothing.

However, ideally you should maintain a blog and several Facebook pages.

Each Facebook page can include a background image that portrays your message. Use these to further reinforce your brand. For example, on my Facebook business page about my book 'How to Sell on eBay', I include a picture of a tropical beach, which triggers thoughts of relaxation, no worries about money, and success.

Once you have created the page, make regular entries of those things that would be of interest to your audience, including photos, graphics, polls, videos, short stories, and anything else that seems appropriate.

As people interact with your content, be sure to answer their questions, acknowledge their statements, and flow with the conversations. This is how you build engagement: you show people that you're knowledgeable, that you care about them, that you have the answers that they're looking for.

Join a multitude of Facebook groups that apply to your message and brand. For example, if you're writing books about Barbie dolls, then search out the Barbie doll groups and join them. Take part in conversations, without promoting, and you'll find that the members will send you friend requests, find out you're an author of books about Barbie dolls, start asking you questions, and at that point they may start purchasing your books.

Exercise: Use Facebook's search bar to find writing groups. Join a few of those and introduce yourself. Start taking part in the conversations by asking questions and getting to know people.

FACEBOOK PROMOTIONAL GROUPS

There are thousands of Facebook groups which specialize in advertising and promoting books. Many of these allow authors to publish promotional posts about their books at any time.

If you visit these groups you'll find page after page of posts with covers and descriptions of books, series, and occasionally other products. These often look like vast catalogs of books being offered for sale by thousands of self-published authors.

Authors post to these on autopilot and are almost never visited by people to buy books, and that makes them useless for book promotion. The authors who are posting their books are not going to buy your books, and the people who are going to buy books are not looking in those groups.

You can find hundreds of gigs (offers to do consulting jobs) on Fiverr.com claiming they can post your book promotion to millions, tens of millions, or even hundreds of millions of people. These gigs post to Facebook (or other social media) groups specializing in publicizing books.

Don't bother. Complete waste of time, and if you personally post too much, Facebook may suspend or close your account.

LINKEDIN PROFILE

> *The first thing you should do as a Social Seller is enhance your LinkedIn profile. Social sellers should make sure they create a good impression before jumping in.* — **Kurt Shaver**

LinkedIn is one of the most important social media platforms for enhancing your brand as an author. Unlike Facebook, LinkedIn is a business social media platform, and everything on it should reflect your professional persona.

If you've already got a LinkedIn profile, go through it with the intent of reworking it to support your brand and your books.

Unlike your author biography, a LinkedIn profile should be written in the first person not the third person. This is because your profile is you telling others about yourself and your specialties.

Everything in the profile should be written to support your niche, your credibility, and the brand that you're trying to build. For example, your educational sections in the profile should include verbiage that describes how your classes and

137

schooling prepared you for your writing career. Each of the positions that you held throughout your life should do the same thing.

The idea is to present a story to those who read your LinkedIn profile which reinforces your credibility and is interesting to those who take the time to read it.

To improve your branding even more, create a company page on LinkedIn to promote your publishing company. You can write a couple of thousand characters about it with some information about your books and so forth.

Your company page can also contain showcase pages. These are very short, each with a paragraph of information about a product or service and a link to a page on your blog. Create one showcase page for each book that you've published, and link to the appropriate descriptive page on Amazon or your blog.

Post an occasional link, short article, video, graphic, or anything else to LinkedIn on a regular schedule. As with Facebook, don't do outright promotion. Your goal is to enlighten your followers to your expertise and knowledge.

Exercise: If you already have a LinkedIn profile, spend some time reviewing it. Does your profile support your career as an author? If you don't have one, then create an account and fill in the blanks in your profile.

GOODREADS

> *Thanks to social media like Facebook, Twitter and Goodreads, I can easily reach out to so many people. Being a writer gives me the added bonus of a targeted audience: readers, who enjoy targeted 'prizes' for participation in fundraisers - books and other neat promo items.* — **Lori Foster**

As an author, it is important for you to be on Goodreads because there are literally tens of millions of readers hanging out there all the time.

http://www.goodreads.com

Join as a member, then follow the directions in this document to create an author profile for yourself.

http://smooth.li/authorprogram

It will take a few days for you to be approved.

Once your Goodreads profile has been created and accepted, explore the interface. In theory, your books should be added to the profile automatically as you publish them on Amazon, but I haven't found that to be true in many instances. In that case, you'll need to contact the Goodreads librarians to help you out. They are a friendly bunch and are happy to help.

The odd thing about Goodreads is that even though it is owned by Amazon, it is run by a group of volunteers, called librarians, who do everything from helping authors with their books to policing for spammers. There doesn't seem to be anyone truly in charge, which can make it frustrating when you need something out of the ordinary.

Chapter 5
Author Platform

As you learn Goodreads, remember it is intended to be a social networking platform for readers. Authors are there to answer questions about their books, and interact with people.

The site is not set up to help authors promote their books, and it is not intended to be used that way – except for paid advertising. You can purchase ads on Goodreads for your books and put them in front of a wide audience of readers.

I have found the best strategy is to treat Goodreads as a social network and not as a marketing, promotional, or advertising tool. Over-promotion can result in permanent bans from the site as well as hostile comments from others.

Spend perhaps an hour a week, at the most, interacting with readers and other authors on Goodreads. Discuss books in your genre, add other people's books to your reading list, and get involved in conversations in areas of interest to you.

Over time, you'll find that you'll be getting more and more attention from readers.

Your main purpose on Goodreads is to gain the attention of those who are popular and review books. If you can succeed in getting your book reviewed by a Goodreads influencer in your field, you will probably gain followers and sales. How do you do that? Find the influencers by reading posts and comments. Start commenting and posting yourself in those threads, and once you've started a dialog with an influencer, mention your book.

The reviews and comments that are left by readers on Goodreads tend to be mildly to extremely harsh. In my experience, books that consistently get four and five-star reviews on Amazon and elsewhere, often get one to three star reviews on Goodreads.

Unlike Amazon, I've also found that ratings are often left without reviews at all. It can be disconcerting to get 4 or 5 one or two-star ratings without any explanation.

It's just the nature of the beast, and it is best to just ignore the comments, reviews, and ratings entirely. They do not carry over to Amazon unless someone manually enters them in both places.

The bottom line is that as an author, it is important for you to be active on Goodreads. However, your ultimate purpose is to help raise your author credibility and let readers get to know you. It will take some time, months or even years, for you to build up a reputation on the social network. This effort will pay off in the long run if you are patient and remember not to do obvious promotion.

Exercise: If you haven't created an account on Goodreads, go ahead and set one up. Explore the site and start interacting with others.

TWITTER

> *If you're on Twitter, what you're saying is, 'I'm important enough for you to care what I think.'* — **Donald Glover**

Some authors swear by Twitter and others swear at Twitter. Spend the time to set up a Twitter account appropriately for your brand. Post on it regularly, and include your Twitter name in all your books, on your social media, and in all your printed materials. Over time, you'll find that you gain followers, and these people are interested in hearing what you have to say.

One of the keys to gaining followers is to follow others. As you follow authors, publishers, readers and so forth, you'll find they follow you back.

Include your Twitter link on your blog, stationary and press kit. Make sure it's easy to find, and you'll discover over time the number of your followers will increase.

There are several businesses that you can pay to help you gain followers. Avoid the temptation to do this, as followers gained in this way are completely useless. They are not engaged with you or your brand as they did not choose to follow you – a computer application made the choice for them. For example, you could pay several hundred dollars to get 100,000 Twitter followers, and yet not even one of those followers would read one of your messages or care about anything you write.

Additionally, purchasing followers violates the terms and conditions of Twitter and your account could be shut down as a result.

I've found that it's difficult to create the kind of relationships you need as an author on Twitter. Messages are short and don't communicate well, and interaction tends to be terse and to the point.

I don't recommend spending a lot of time on Twitter, except to post everything you create, including videos, articles, audio, and images to your Twitter feed.

Exercise: If you don't have a Twitter account, then set one up now. Follow some people you know and read their feeds.

YOUTUBE

Humans are incredibly visual and powerful, moving images help us find meaning… [and] video helps capture and contextualize the world around us. — **Dan Patterson**

YouTube is one of the most important social media platforms for authors. Create a YouTube channel dedicated for videos related to your author brand. Keep this separate from your personal YouTube channel.

Any videos that you create, such as an author biography video, explainer video, book trailers, and video reviews should be posted to your author channel. Share them on your other social media such as Facebook and Google Plus as well as your blog.

If you're going to go to the trouble of creating a YouTube channel to help promote you as an author, then be sure to keep it regularly updated with new videos. A video a week, or at least one every other week, is a good goal.

Your videos don't have to be professionally produced. A quick five-minute clip of you talking about one of your books at a book signing would be great for this purpose. If you give a talk or other event related to your book, then take as much video as you possibly can. You can edit those down to small video spots and use them as needed to help promote yourself.

What about using video sites such as Vimeo? There are many excellent video hosting sites. Some are free and some come at a cost. The advantages of YouTube are that it's free, the quality is high, and **Google favors YouTube videos in its search algorithms**.

How about loading videos to Facebook? This is another great idea, and it is true that Facebook favors videos that it hosts over those from other sites. One strategy is to host your videos on BOTH sites: YouTube and Facebook. Use the YouTube videos for everywhere except Facebook.

Exercise: Set up your author YouTube channel. Explore the various settings and read the help files and tutorials.

PINTEREST AND INSTAGRAM

> *When people hear information, they're likely to remember only 10% of that information three days later. However, if a relevant image is paired with that same information, people retained 65% of the information three days later.* — **John Medina** (Medina 2015)

These two social media platforms are centered on images. If the topic of your book or your genre lends itself to being portrayed visually, then these, and similar ones, will work well for you.

They seem to be popular for recipes, hobbies, coloring books, art, photography, and any other subject that can be graphically portrayed.

Whatever you post will be reposted all over the web by potentially hundreds of thousands of people. If you post the uncolored coloring pages directly from your coloring books, you'll find people stealing them rather than buying your books.

Unless you purchase a third-party tool, you'll need to use a smartphone or similar device to post photos and images to Instagram. For an author, posting photos of the creative process, interviews, book signings, and activities can be successful. Keep your smartphone handy, and if something in your environment seems pertinent, then snap a photo and upload it to Instagram.

For Pinterest, photos and images must be added one at a time from a computer or from your smartphone and similar devices.

Both visual social networks require constant attention to be successful. For example, on Pinterest, you need to pin 20 to 50 images every day at different times. Pinning that many images all at once will not be nearly as successful.

Exercise: If you haven't already, create your Instagram and Pinterest accounts.

Chapter 5
Author Platform

AUTOMATION

> *The first rule of any technology used in a business is that automation applied to an efficient operation will magnify the efficiency. The second is that automation applied to an inefficient operation will magnify the inefficiency.* — **Bill Gates**

Automation of social media is a tricky subject. The problem all authors face is that there is only so much time in a day, and only so many days in a week. Social media can be a huge burden, especially if it's not done correctly or optimally.

Many courses recommend using automation to help reduce the burden of maintaining social media for authors, while at the same time increasing the amount of work done.

The idea is that it keeps your name and your brand in front of your readers. There is some merit to this concept, and it can be effective, but I question its true value.

The problem is that the purpose of social media is to create relationships with your readers, and I haven't found any automation yet that can do that. Sure, it can help by alleviating the burden of some posting (especially by spreading it out through the day or week) but the actual interaction still requires human intervention.

Automated software, such as HootSuite and MassPlanner, can certainly post whatever you want on a scheduled basis for days, months, or even years in advance. But blindly throwing mud on the wall doesn't usually produce results, and just creates random noise that annoys people.

https://hootsuite.com/

http://www.massplanner.com/

Automation is not intelligent, because it just dumps information into your social media newsfeeds without concern about whether it's pertinent, interesting, engaging, relevant, or even important.

Unless well-planned, automated posts do not create an interaction with your readers and followers. In fact, it is usually obvious when a post has been automatically injected into a newsfeed, as opposed to having been written by a real human being.

One school of thought is to create a different quote along with the graphic and your website name for every single day for a six-month timeframe. You then schedule these quotes in your automated software, kick back, put your feet on the desk, and be happy that you don't have to do that manually anymore.

You'll find this has no effect because there's no interaction. Without interaction, there is no engagement.

You don't need or want to overwhelm your followers by posting what is basically useless junk – most people call it spam – repeatedly. Regardless of whether automation is used or not, posting for the sake of posting has no value at all and wastes time and effort.

A good use of automated software is to post, on a regular basis, relevant information that is helpful to your readers. In other words, you might create a schedule to post a separate training video to your newsfeed on Facebook once a week for 24 weeks. At the end of that time, the automation starts over from the first video. This gives your readers some useful information and may strengthen your brand dramatically.

Focus on creating 'evergreen' materials (meaning they are not date sensitive). These can be short training videos, images, stories, testimonials, or infographics. As you finish these, then add them as appropriate to your automation.

At some point, as you write and publish more books, you're going to run out of time in the day. You'll find that you can't get everything you need to get done completed, and the problem will get worse and worse as time goes on.

Automation can help with this, but it cannot replace the human factor. Use automation wisely and it can help you reinforce your brand and engage with the readers. Use it unwisely, not only will you be wasting your time, but will almost certainly alienate readers who will ignore your message. And ultimately, you will be tarnishing your author cred, which is not easy to recover from.

Outsourcing

> *If you deprive yourself of outsourcing and your competitors do not, you're putting yourself out of business.* — **Lee Kuan Yew**

Outsourcing (hiring others to do work for you) is a great idea for many tasks, and it can work with your social media campaigns. There are several ways to hire people to get things done for you, including virtual assistants and professional companies.

Virtual assistants are consultants who work over the web from anywhere in the world. You can find these on Fiverr.com, you can visit ivaa.org (International Virtual Assistants Association) or you can look any number of other places.

http://ivaa.org

You can find virtual assistants (consultants who work over the internet) to do just about anything for you – if you can define it so they understand what to do. Generally, the best tactic is to perform the task yourself for a while, create an easy-to-follow script, and give that to your virtual assistant.

A virtual assistant can help immensely with your social media campaign. You shouldn't expect them to do any kind of creative work, respond to comments, or design anything for you. Their purpose is to do some of the mundane, repeatable tasks that take up large amounts of time.

For example, with Pinterest it's best to post pins throughout the day. This can be very time-consuming and can interrupt your routine. You could create the pins (images) then send to a virtual assistant who can take care of the task of posting them for you over a longer period of time.

Hiring professional firms to do a social media campaign can be expensive and is often a shot in the dark. I've been quoted rates starting at $1,500 a month from one social media company to "build my brand" on LinkedIn alone. They required a six-month contract, meaning the campaign would cost $9,000 with no guarantee of success.

Even if you can find professionals that you can afford, they may have a difficult time coming up with the appropriate content and interacting with your followers and readers unless they understand your market and message well.

This is not to say that hiring a professional to do the work for you is out of the question – you're just going to have to work closely with them, monitor their progress, and expect to pay premium rates. Professionals in this area, at least if they're any good, don't come cheap.

In my experience, the best use of professionals is to hire them as advisors who help come up with ideas and concepts to use for example in a campaign, and then help design that campaign.

TYING IT ALL TOGETHER

The trap of social media is that it can become a black hole for time without any significant resulting sales. It can be very frustrating to be going through the motions for hours every single day, only to get one or two sales out of it all.

The idea is to find a balance of social media that works for you and your brand and the message you are trying to portray without it becoming a time rathole.

Following is a summary of the various platforms that authors can use to get their message out, in order of importance.

Author blog – Create and maintain a blog, preferably using WordPress under your own domain name. The blog is your home base and everything should point back to it.

Email list – Create an email list, and actively pursue sign-ups, so that you can stay in touch with your readers.

YouTube Channel – YouTube videos are an excellent way to stay in contact and update your readers at a relatively low cost in time and money. You can create a video in a very short time using a smartphone or the webcam on your desktop or laptop, which can be posted to your blog and social media. Producing a video a week, or two a month, doesn't take a lot of time and keeps your readers engaged.

Facebook – Facebook is the most important social media platform for engaging with readers, because virtually everyone is on Facebook every day, several times a week, or at least once a month. In fact, most people have Facebook installed on their desktop, cell phone, tablet, and everything else they own.

Create a Facebook page for you as an author and then another one for each of your major efforts – perhaps your most significant book or two, and your book series. Use these to stay in contact with your readers, as well as posting your

Chapter 5
Author Platform

YouTube videos and blog articles as appropriate on each page.

LinkedIn – Create a LinkedIn profile, ensure it is professional and that it shows your career progression and how you became an author. Once you get the profile created, you don't need to spend a lot of time on LinkedIn. Half an hour a week is more than enough time to post a few status updates, add a picture, comment on a few things, and make a change here or there.

Twitter – Create a Twitter account, and post links to any articles that you write on your blog, any videos that you post to your YouTube channel, and anything important that you add to your Facebook pages.

Make sure your Twitter handle is printed on all your written materials and stationary, on the contact page of your blog, and everywhere else visible to your readers.

Don't spend a lot of time with Twitter, just post things that are of interest to your audience and engage with your followers occasionally.

Pinterest and Instagram – If your topic lends itself to visual portrayals, such as recipe or coloring books, then you should be using Pinterest and Instagram to promote your works. As with all the other social media platforms, post for engagement, not for its own sake.

For example, if you publish coloring books, then you might post colored images of each page to your Pinterest and Instagram accounts.

Goodreads – Goodreads is an important social media platform for authors, but it's one of the most difficult to use effectively. Out of all the various platforms, this is the one that tolerates self-promotion by authors the least. The best strategy is to create your author profile on Goodreads, and from that point on, forget you are an author and just take part in the conversations as a reader of other people's books. Eventually your books will get discovered by popular reviewers, which will result in increased sales.

Google Plus – I haven't talked about Google Plus because I haven't found it to be an effective platform for authors. You may want to experiment with this platform and decide for yourself if it works for you.

TIME

Wow, that sure seems overwhelming, doesn't it?

Take it a little at a time. Building your author platform, which is a mixture of everything mentioned in this chapter and more, is not something that happens overnight, in a month, or even in a year.

Start with your blog and email list, and then move through the social media that makes sense to you. You could start from where you spend the most time every day. For example, if you're on Facebook constantly, then that would be a great place to begin after you have created your blog and email list.

On the other hand, if you enjoy making videos, then, by all means, head on over to YouTube, create a channel, and have fun with it.

Chapter 5
Author Platform

But remember your main mission: which is to write and publish books and promote those to your audience. Social media is a tool to help you do that.

In other words, treat social media as a means to an end. Don't let yourself get sucked into posting endlessly and mindlessly or merely for the sake of posting itself. After you've created your profiles, pages and groups – in other words once you've set up the basics – limit your interaction to less than an hour each day if possible.

CONCLUSIONS

One of the most delightful parts of being a writer is connecting with people via social media. I devote ten minutes out of every writing hour to Twitter, Facebook, Goodreads, LinkedIn, Pinterest, and other sites. I don't use assistants for that. It's me and all of my friends, fans, readers, and colleagues on the crazyboat. — **Jonathan Maberry**

An author platform is one of the most important long-term components of your career as a self-published author. This is the way you communicate to your readers, and other writers, agents, reviewers, and anyone else who was interested in you and your works.

Begin by creating a blog, even if only a simple one, which gives you a home base for all your other materials and information. Just as important, create your email list so that you can start collecting subscribers. Include a sign-up form on your blog and, if you have one, the related Facebook page.

Once you've done that, define a Facebook business page and a LinkedIn profile, and then proceed to Goodreads and set yourself up as an author.

Spend some time, perhaps a few months, getting into the groove of maintaining regular updates to these outlets. As you get more time, and become more motivated, you might go ahead and create a monthly or weekly podcast of your own, do a few book signings, and maybe even do some public speaking.

It's tempting to post the same information to these different social media platforms into your blog. You should avoid this temptation and post different things to each platform. Put together a weekly schedule to help you control all the activity that you need to perform.

For example, you might post an update to Facebook three times a week on Monday, Thursday, and Saturday; write a blog entry on Sunday; and post to LinkedIn every Wednesday. Finally, you may spend 30 minutes twice a week working on Goodreads.

A word of caution: Social media can become an addictive time-zapper, if not controlled properly. It's easy to get caught up in long conversations because it's fun to communicate with readers and other interested parties.

That's why it's important to create a schedule with specific parameters of when and how much time you spend on each social media platform. Even more importantly, commit and stick to it.

Chapter 6
Your Author Blog

One of the most vital components of your author platform is your author blog. This gives you a place to call home on the internet, anchors your credibility, and helps to sell your books over the long-term.

You don't have to spend a lot of time working on it initially, at least not until you have a few books under your belt. However, it's a good idea to purchase the hosting and domain name, install WordPress, and set up a very basic blog to begin with. This will at least allow you to refer people to your site within your book, during conversations, and in your advertisements.

You can take the time to learn more about how to blog, maintain WordPress, and write articles later when you have more availability. Once you've got your blog set up, write an article a week and post links to it on different days to all your social media.

This chapter overviews the purpose and some of the basics about an author blog. The final section, Recommended Courses, lists a few short online courses that will help you understand how to work with WordPress.

Chapter 6
Your Author Blog

WHY YOU MUST HAVE A BLOG

> *Put your blog out into the world and hope that your talent will speak for itself.* — **Diablo Cody**

A blog serves as your headquarters or your home base. This is where you'll write any articles about you and your works, post pictures, include links to videos, and so forth.

Get a personalized domain name for your blog and email address. Many authors get a domain name that is their own name, such as richardlowe.com, while others get something that identifies them such as the name of their business or book series.

If you'd rather not use WordPress, you can quickly create a simple blog on sites such as wix.com, web.com, or blogger.com and then forward your domain to it.

Forwarding a domain name is simple in concept. Let's say your blog is damiansmith.web.com. Purchase your domain name, for example damiansmith.com, and set it up within your domain registrar to forward to damiansmith.web.com. The help desk at the registrar will be able to help you set this up.

I host my blogs on Siteground, and they have proven to be rock-solid stable and very high performing. The first-year of hosting will cost around fifty bucks, and that includes a free domain name. After one year, it will cost a little more, but hopefully by then you will be making enough money where that's not an issue.

http://smooth.li/siteground
Note, this is an affiliate link. If you purchase the product I will receive a small commission.

This might seem intimidating, at least at first, but it is necessary if you want to build your brand as an author and increase your income. You almost certainly won't make any money directly off your blog, but merely by the fact of having one and keeping it updated, you'll give your readers a place to visit to find out about you, read about your books, learn what you're going to do in the future, and join your email list.

It's not a good idea to use social media such as Facebook as your "home base" because you lose control of your content. You could spend a lot of effort to build up a following on Facebook (or other social media) only to find it gone because you accidentally violated one of their terms, a hacker broke in and deleted your page, or some other calamity happens.

If possible, spend the money to purchase hosting and create a professional blog using WordPress. If you don't how to do that, then you can either hire someone to help you, or find a person in your network who has WordPress experience and trade services — for example, you might be able to write them copy for their website in exchange for creating a WordPress site for you.

Initially, your blog doesn't have to be complicated. A front page, about section, contact page, and a few articles are all that you need to get going.

It's important to use paid hosting so that your blog belongs to you. If you're using free hosting, your content is at the mercy of the hosting site. For example, years ago, there was a major hosting company called GeoCities — over 38 million sites were hosted there. In October 2009, Yahoo shut down GeoCities and those sites disappeared forever. See the Wikipedia article Yahoo! GeoCities for more information.

https://en.wikipedia.org/wiki/Yahoo!_GeoCities

Additionally, most web hosts include fully functional email accounts with the hosting service.

The support people in your hosting company's support group will be happy to help you if you have any trouble setting things up or if you have questions. I called Siteground's technical support several times while setting up my blog, and they usually picked up the call on the third ring and had the answer to me within a few minutes.

You should plan to post at least something every week on your blog. An article a week is a great pace to keep your readers engaged. However, keep posts regular, because nothing chases away followers – who are your potential clients and readers – faster than a blog, or any type of posting, which hasn't been updated in a long time.

In summary, take the time to learn how to create a blog, and keep it up-to-date. If you can, spend the money to get professional web hosting from a company such as Siteground and create the blog using WordPress. Make sure you get a domain name, such as your name, to make it easy for people to find you.

I know this all sounds a bit complicated, but believe me, over the long term it's well worth the effort.

DOMAIN NAME

A domain name is your address, your address on the Internet. We all have a physical address; we're all going to need an address in cyberspace. They're becoming increasingly important. I believe we'll get to the point where when you're born, you'll be issued a domain name. — **Bob Parsons**

When you create your blog, whether you use Siteground.com or another host, make sure you get a domain name to go with it. Usually, when you purchase web hosting, you'll get one free with the first year of service.

Regardless of whether you want to confront the complexities of using WordPress, purchase a customized domain name. This allows you to use that in your books and promotional materials, and makes it easier to move a WordPress blog to a different host later if that's what you decide to do. If you don't get a customized domain name, if you move your blog, you'll have to change every reference to it in all your books, social media, and elsewhere.

You should pick a domain name that reinforces your brand, which brings to life the image you want to portray in your reader's minds.

For example, one of my domain names is thewritingking.com which matches the name of my blog and the image that I wish to transmit. I have another domain name called thecoloringking.com which is for my line of coloring books, which reinforces that brand.

This domain name is important because you'll use it for your email address as well as your blog, for example rich@thewritingking.com.

Once you have your blog, email, and domain name set up, then include that domain name on your business cards, invoices, letterhead, email signature, and anywhere else that is seen by your customers, readers, vendors, or others. The idea is that everything points back to your blog, because that is your home base.

As an example, if you had written a series of fiction novels about intelligent dragons, you might create a brand called "Intelligent Dragons". Your domain name, assuming it's available, could be intelligentdragons.com. Combined with a well-designed dragon logo, this would be a very powerful and memorable brand.

FRONT PAGE

The front page of your blog is vital, and the section that is "above the fold" (the top of the page that is visible on the screen) is the most important part of that.

On the image below, the sidebar is the gray box on the left. This typically contains a menu (a way to choose where to go in the site), your logo, and a link to your signup form.

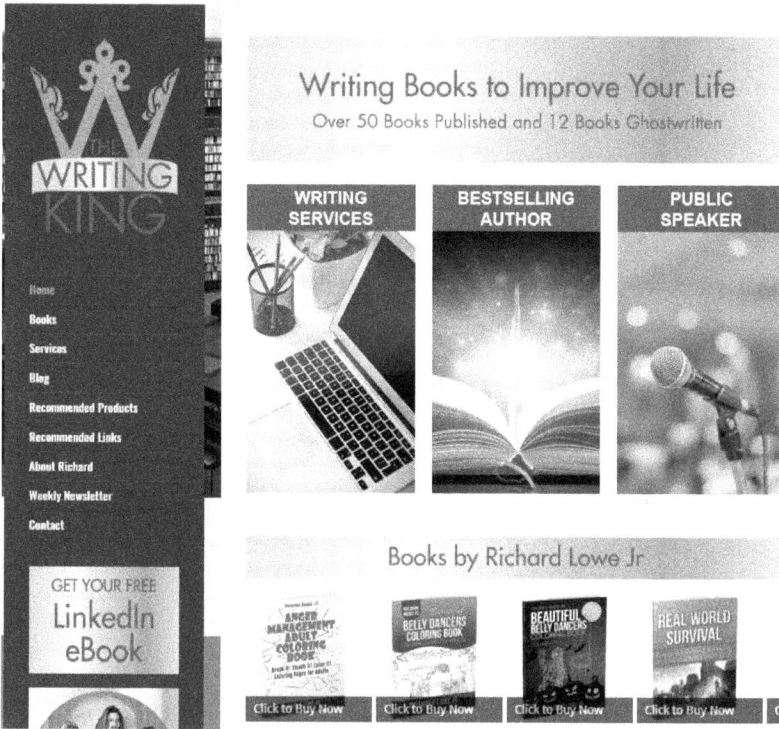

On my front page, clicking on either of the three large boxes (Writing Services, Bestselling Author, or Public Speaker) brings the visitor to a page describing and expanding on each of those topics.

Keep your front page simple and easy to navigate. The less clutter the better.

It's a good idea to include your picture above the fold if you can, as well as the links to all your books, or book series. When someone visits your author site they want to see you and your books before anything else.

Make sure the colors, fonts, and style portray the image you are trying to project.

ABOUT PAGE

The About Page tells your readers about yourself or your company. This is the long version of your author biography. Generally, this is written in the third-person (like someone is telling your reader about you). Includes a few pictures or drawings of yourself so your readers get to see who you are.

As you can see from the screenshot from my website (below), the sidebar on the about page is the same as the sidebar on the front page of the website.

Spend the time to make your 'About' Page fantastic. You'll find it is one of the most visited pages on your blog.

CONTACT PAGE

You must include a contact page on your blog. This is how people get a hold of you.

Use a form to collect their email address, name, and a message. Don't ask them for more information than that. All you need is a way to get back to them and their message.

Also, don't put your email address, phone number, or home address out on the web. Let them contact you through your form.

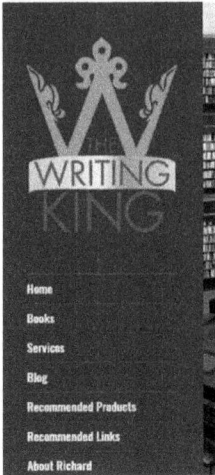

MEDIA PAGE

The purpose of a Media Page is to give members of the press, podcasters, producers and others the information they will need for their articles or shows.

Keep your media page simple to begin with and add to it over time as you gain experience and credentials. Spend the time to make sure it's right, accurate and promotes you well.

Include the following:

- A biography, written in the third person.
- Several professional photos (up to 4).
- An introduction to be used for speaking engagements.
- The answers to a few sample interview questions.
- The contact information for your publicist if appropriate.
- A list of your books, articles and other materials.

It's common for the media page to be one of the most heavily accesses pages on a blog.

RECOMMENDED PLUGINS

In WordPress, you can install many applications called plug-ins, each of which allows you to modify the behavior of your blog. There are tens of thousands of plug-ins available to do every conceivable thing, and there are a few that are especially useful on an author blog.

It's beyond the scope of this book to go into any of these plug-ins in any significant detail. This is a list of those that I find most useful, and I'm including them so that you can investigate them further and use them they appeal to you.

Contact Form 7 – (Free) A simple contact form which you can use to get names, email addresses, and messages (among other things).

Mooberry Book Manager – (Free) An excellent plugin that lets you set up book pages, book lists, and so forth. The main plug-in is free, and there are four additional plug-ins to let you do even more.

Meta Slider – (Free) A nice plug-in that let you define a slider to show off your books. I've installed this on my front page to show off all my books.

Social Media Feather – (Free) This includes buttons at the bottom of every post and page to let people share them with their friends on Facebook, Twitter, and other social media.

WP-SpamShield – (Free) Helps to keep your blog safe and free of spam.

Yoast SEO – (Free) This excellent plug-in helps you tune your site so that the search engines are more likely to include it in their index.

Once you learn the power of plug-ins, it's very tempting to go overboard and install dozens, or even hundreds of them to do every conceivable thing. You can think of them like building blocks for blogs.

Resist the temptation to install more than a dozen, or at the most two dozen, because every one of them affects the security and performance of your blog. Also, avoid installing any plug-in that has not been tested on your current version, even if they seem to work, and any of them that have more than a few recent negative reviews.

Don't worry if you don't know any of this means right now. If you don't understand WordPress, either hire someone who does, or take some of the courses recommended in the following section. Not to worry, you don't need to install any plug-ins at all to begin with.

RECOMMENDED COURSES

Below are listed some courses on Udemy.com that can help you learn the basics of WordPress and blogging.

Blogging for Authors and Newbies on WordPress or Blogger

http://smooth.li/udemy-blogging
Note, this is an affiliate link. If you purchase the product I will receive a small commission.

WordPress for Beginners 2016-Perfect for authors & bloggers

http://smooth.li/udemy-beginners
Note, this is an affiliate link. If you purchase the product I will receive a small commission.

Wordpress For Authors

http://smooth.li/udemy-authors
Note, this is an affiliate link. If you purchase the product I will receive a small commission.

CONCLUSIONS

The most important component of your author platform is your blog. This gives you a place on the Internet that you can call home and use as a reference point for your readers and other interested people.

Chapter 6
Your Author Blog

Keep your blog up to date, and post to it often – at least once a week. Everything about you, your books, and your series should be available to a visitor to your blog.

WordPress is the best platform for your blog because it is simple and there are many themes (blueprints for how your blog looks) and plug-ins available, so you can customize it to be exactly what you want.

Once you've got your blog up and running, even in the simplified version, the next thing to create and build up for your author platform is your email list.

Chapter 7
Your Email List

> *You can think of the names on your email list as customers asking for you to send them things to purchase.*

In its simplest form, an email list is a list of the names and email addresses of people so that you can occasionally send out information to them.

In this chapter, we will be briefly discussing email lists that allow you to automate sign-ups, email campaigns, and unsubscribe, as a minimum.

The reason why these lists are so important is that they are comprised of people who asked to receive information from you. That implies that they are interested in what you have to say, which means they are qualified leads.

One of your major goals as you market your books and yourself, is to get people to sign up to your email list and to send out letters (email messages) to them on a regular basis.

LEAD MAGNETS

> *A small list that wants exactly what you're offering is better than a bigger list that isn't committed. — **Ramsay Leimenstoll***

To attract people to joining your list, create what's called a lead magnet. This is also referred to as an 'ethical bribe' by some marketers.

Chapter 7
Your Email List

The idea is to give away something for free – it must be valuable – to entice people into subscribing. These gifts can be virtually anything: a PDF file, a checklist, an interview, a video, or something else that has perceived value.

For example, my lead magnet for my coloring book email list is a sample containing one coloring page from some of the coloring books that I've published – a total of 8 pages. That's a good freebie, and it entices a lot of people into subscribing.

If you wrote a book about LinkedIn, you might give away a checklist for setting up a LinkedIn profile. Fiction authors often give away the first chapter or two of their books, or at times, even an entire book which serves as a very good lead magnet.

After you have finish creating your lead magnet, set up a form on your blog which accepts a name and email address. Don't ask for anything more than that, as the more information you request, the less people are going to be inclined to sign-up. This form is generally provided by your email autoresponder service provider, a few of which are listed and described in the next section.

Inside your books, include as much as a page at the front and a page at the back, describing your free product along with a link to your golden email list signup page.

Exercise: Think about your book. What kind of lead magnet would make sense to get people to subscribe to your mailing list? Think about the following:

- For a novel, a short prequel would be a great freebie, and will also set up the scene for your novel.

- For non-fiction, a checklist, a video tutorial, or even a rolodex of contact is a great freebie.

What kind of freebie makes sense for your book or book series?

SERVICES

To automate your email list, you need to choose an autoresponder service. Three of the best services are listed below.

MailChimp – A good entry-level service is MailChimp. You can begin using the service for free, and as your list grows and you need more features, paid options are available. Their automation, available in the paid option, is excellent, and allows you a lot of ways to service your list.

http://smooth.li/mailchimp

Aweber – Aweber is a top-of-the-line autoresponder provider. They also have a free version available, and provide paid upgrade options. They can handle lists of all sizes, but their options are more complex and more suitable for advanced users.

http://smooth.li/aweber
Note, this is an affiliate link. If you purchase the product I will receive a small commission.

TrafficWave - The advantage of TrafficWave is that it offers a fixed-price regardless of the size of your list. For under $20 a month, they provide all the functionality that most authors will need.

http://smooth.li/trafficwave

Exercise: Visit each of the sites above and read the descriptions thoroughly. Which of them appears to be best for you? Then sign up for a free account on MailChimp and experiment with the options available.

AUTORESPONDER SEQUENCES

Once you've selected a service, read their documentation thoroughly and start creating your autoresponder sequences.

An autoresponder sequence is a list of email messages sent to each subscriber within a certain time and order. For example, look at the list below:

- Immediately after subscribing: send a welcome message.
- One day later: introduce yourself with a short biography.
- Three days after that: send an article describing why you became an author.
- Three days after that: send a list of your books.
- And so forth…

The idea is that this is all handled automatically. Your job is to create the lead magnet and the letters (email messages) that are sent to your subscribers. You can have as many email messages as you like and you can define the amount of time in between mailings. They can span one day, several days, weeks, or even months apart.

What do you send out? Treat it the same as you do your social media. In other words, you are trying to build a relationship with your email list. Send your subscribers information that is consistently as valuable as possible.

For example, you could create a course on how to do something, and split it up into 10 different messages in your autoresponder sequence. For fiction authors, you could send out chapters or snippets from your various works. Coloring book publishers might send out a free page now and then for people to color.

Be careful sending out too much that is free. You train your list by what you send. If you consistently give away too much for free, then you'll find your list doesn't buy very much. In other words, only occasionally give away things for free, if at all.

Your email list is more or less a way to stay engaged with your readers and those that asked to be on your list are generally more interested in what you have to say because they asked to be there.

Exercise: MailChimp has some great tutorials on how to do email campaigns. Look through them to get more information on how you can use this tool.

Chapter 7
Your Email List

OCCASIONAL MESSAGES

In addition to your automated (canned) messages, you should also occasionally send to your list to inform them about things that are going on.

For example:

- When you publish a new book.
- If you are giving a speech or a book signing.
- If you are featured in a media event such as a television interview.
- If you win an award or are highly honored.
- And other, similar events.

Don't send these unscheduled messages too often; once a month is probably about right, and once a week might be too often (it depends on yours).

These keep the people on your list informed of what is going on with you, which is presumably why they subscribed to your list in the first place.

DON'T OVERDO IT

Understand that your email list is a marketing tool to stay in contact with your readers and keep them engaged with your brand.

It is not an advertising tool. Affiliate marketers use their email lists as advertising tools, and they typically send out an email as often as every day of the week with a new product or service for sale.

As you proceed through the world of becoming a self-published author, you'll run into these affiliate marketers. Typically, this happens when you sign-up for a webinar that sounds interesting. These webinars are infomercials in disguise and their purpose is to sell one or more products.

Yes, the webinars are generally useful, and you can gain valuable information just by listening to them. However, the whole idea is to give you enough information to prove to you that what is being sold has value, and to intellectually and emotionally pull you in and cause you to make a purchase.

Your author email list is not the same thing, though. Your purpose is to increase the engagement of your readers so that they purchase your books and other products over time.

One or two email messages per week is more than enough to maintain engagement with your readers.

You can also send an occasional message manually when you have something new to tell your readers, such as a book that's been published or an event that you'll be attending. Since these are not evergreen, you would not include them in your autoresponder sequence.

The danger of sending too many messages is that you will alienate your readers. Your messages will be ignored, deleted, or reported as spam.

If you send too few messages, less than one every other week, your readers will forget about you and your engagement will weaken.

Chapter 7
Your Email List

Conclusions

An email list is an essential part of your author platform. It enables you to remain in contact with your most engaged fans and readers. Combined with your blog and the other social media platforms that work for you, you'll be able to build excitement about your books which, in turn, will lead to increased sales.

If you don't use an email list effectively, you're losing out on the best way to stay connected with your readers.

There are many more techniques that you can use to take full advantage of an email list. If you read through the documentation of the autoresponder services, you can get an idea of just how many possibilities there are.

Since your goal is just to remain engaged with your most fervent readers, my advice is to keep your email list simple. Add a message a week to your autoresponder sequence, and send out an occasional message to announce something. That's about as complex as you'll need most of the time.

Remember that more complexity requires more of your time to maintain which means you'll be spending less time writing, publishing and engaging with your readers on social media and blog. Keep it simple and you'll be fine.

Chapter 8
Legal Concerns

> *I am not a lawyer, and the information is this section is intended for only for general guidance. On each of these topics, you should consult an attorney and do your own research.*

Many writers, especially those who are just starting out, are not cognizant of some of the legal concerns associated with publishing and writing books. After all, in the United States at least, "it's a free country", isn't it? We do have freedom of speech, the press and expression, don't we?

It is true that legally you can write and publish just about anything you want, with some restrictions.

Copyright laws protect the works of authors (and others) by making it illegal for people to copy the creations of others without permission. If this law didn't exist, then anything you created could be taken by other people, who could make money off it, leaving you without proper without compensation, let alone recognition for what you've accomplished.

Fair use is an exception to the copyright law that allows people to use small quotes or parts of copyrighted works for things like quotes and movie reviews as well as paraphrasing in research papers and the like.

Companies create trademarks to protect their brands, and there are restrictions on the use of those trademarks in written works. Primarily, if you use a trademark you must not cause confusion about the brand. For example, if you wrote a book about MacDonald's, you must not make it seem like it was approved or authorized them (unless, of course, it was).

Finally, you cannot libel or slander (defame in writing or orally) another person (unless they're dead). To defame someone is to communicate untruths that portray them negatively.

Each of these concepts and the restrictions that they place upon your writing is discussed in the section.

COPYRIGHT

People work hard to develop graphics, write stories and articles, design web sites and build software, and other things. They are sometimes paid for their efforts, sometimes not. In any event, in the United States (and in most of the world) any original work that you create is automatically protected by copyright.

You can find out more about copyright law in the United States here:

https://www.copyright.gov/

You do not need to register your works with the copyright office for them to be protected[7]. Registration serves as added insurance – it gives you the ability to prove that you wrote or

---

[7] This is true in the United States. If you reside in other countries, check out the law for your area.

created your work on a specific date and formally establishes you as the copyright owner.

A person or company owns the rights to publish the material. These rights continue regardless of how many times the material is illegally copied, given away or sold by the copyright owner.

Note that you can grant others limited rights to your works, such as the right to display an image, or to use your book as the basis for a movie.

Using someone's images, writings, songs (MP3's included), videos or anything else without permission (except for fair use) is violating the law and the person's rights. In fact, it is stealing (although not in a criminal sense) and, if proven, the violator can be held liable for losses and/or damages.

What should you do when you want to use a few paragraphs or pages from someone else's material? Well, you can write to the copyright owner and ask permission. Get permission in writing because oral agreements are difficult or impossible to enforce in a court of law.

I've found that most artists and writers on the internet are willing to allow their work to be copied if they get credit and a citation or compensation.

Some examples of behaviors that violate copyright law in the United States are:

Taking images from newsgroups. Just because something has been copied to a newsgroup, regardless of whether the copy was made by the copyright owner or someone else, does not mean that the copyright has been given up.

Using articles and images from other web sites. Again, this is illegal unless explicit permission is given, or the item in question is in the public domain. However, you can link to anything on the web without permission; linking does not violate any United States laws.

Scanning images from magazines and books. This is illegal as you are making a copy (a scan) of a copyrighted work.

Modifying an image and claiming it as your own. Copyright protects derivations of works as well.

On the other hand, the following are acceptable under the US copyright laws.

Including a few brief quotes from a book in a review. This is acceptable under fair use laws. Include a citation to give credit to the source.

Reprinting or copying parts from a confirmed public domain novel.

Asking and obtaining reprint permission. If you get permission from the copyright owner or their legal agent, you are fine. Be sure to get permission in writing.

Reading an article about cheese puffs and writing your own article about cheese puffs. Copyright protects creative works and any derivations made from them, but not ideas or concepts.

When in doubt, ask permission. If you are denied permission or for some reason cannot obtain it, then don't use the material.

And always cite your sources.

FAIR USE

In order to include quotes of another author's works, an exemption to the United States copyright law was created. This allows for "commentary, parody, news reporting, research and education about copyrighted works without the permission of the author" (Templeton 2008).

So how does this work? Well, some of the more important considerations are:

- Your intent in copying the work.
- How much of the work was copied?
- As well as any damage to the commercial value of the original work.

For example, if you write an article about the quality of the movie "The Mummy Returns", you could use brief quotes from the film to illustrate your point. However, if you included the entire script (or significant portions of it), then that would be a copyright violation.

Chapter 8
Legal Concerns

It is a good idea to include a reference (citation) to the original source material. This gives your readers the opportunity to look at the source document for additional information. You add to your credibility by showing you have done your research.

To further illustrate, the following would most likely be covered under fair use:

- Including brief quotes from published papers for your research papers.
- Reviewing a book and including a few quotes to illustrate your point.
- Reviewing a book and including quotes from other critics to reinforce your point.

The following would most likely be considered copyright violations:

- Including, without permission, several pages of material from another research paper.
- Wholesale copying of pages from a website to your book.
- Scanning photographs of Heather Locklear from Cosmopolitan and using them in your book or website.

You can find out more about fair use here:

http://smooth.li/fairuse

TRADEMARKS

Trademarks are words, phrases, or graphics that have been reserved by businesses or individuals for their own use. Typically, these are product names, logos, short phrases and things like that that are used in branding a business or individual.

A service mark is a trademark that applies to a business or company that provides services, and is often referred to as a trademark.

In the United States, trademarks are not required to be registered, but it is a good idea because it gives notice to the public that a business has exclusive rights to the trademark.

Protection for trademarks comes in using the mark to identify your goods or services, not in registering the trademark with the USPTO (US Patent and Trademark Office).

A business that uses a trademark could lose protection of that trademark if they fail to enforce their rights. This means that if you, the author of a book, infringe upon a trademark, then the owner of that trademark *must* enforce the rights by demanding that you to stop using it.

This doesn't mean you can't reference trademarks inside of your books. You can do so if you're not infringing upon that trademark.

TRADEMARKS IN THE TEXT
There are a few areas that you need to be concerned about as a writer if you use trademarks.

Chapter 8
Legal Concerns

Infringement - Trademark infringement is an unauthorized use of the mark that creates the likelihood of confusion about the product or services. For example, if a company created an airplane called Boeing, then the Boeing Corporation would likely demand that they stop using that name for their product.

Dilution - If you use a trademark in a generic way, such as referring to 'photocopying' as a 'xeroxing', this dilutes the trademark because it makes it more generic instead of specific to the brand.

Defamation – This is falsely depicting a trademark product or service in a negative light. For example, if you wrote a fiction story about Coca-Cola® killing people straight out of the bottle, you might get a sternly worded letter from that company. In this case, it is better to use a fictional brand name to protect yourself.

The long and short of it is if you use trademarks in a respectful way and formatted the way that it should be formatted, you should be fine. For example, if you're going to reference eBay, make sure you spell and capitalize the word exactly right. In this case, the "E" is lowercase and the "B" is uppercase.

If you're being respectful about the use of the trade or service marks, you shouldn't have any problem using them in your books. The exception is on the book cover, title, subtitle and series name.

COPYRIGHT PAGE NOTICE

If you use trademarks within your book, it's a good idea to add a disclaimer to your copyright page. A sample is shown below.

> *Trademarked names appear throughout this book. Rather than use a trademark symbol with every occurrence of a trademarked name, names are used in an editorial fashion, with no intention of infringement of the respective owner's trademark.*

A notice such as this just spells out that you don't have any intent of infringing on anyone's trademark.

TRADEMARKS IN THE BOOK TITLE

The problem with using a trademark in your book title is that a reader could be confused as to whether your book was officially authorized or not. To protect their trademarks, businesses must enforce their usage. They do this by sending out cease-and-desist letters, and in extreme cases, filing lawsuits.

Before including the name of any business, product or service in your title, subtitle or book cover do a search on the web to ensure that someone hasn't registered that trademark.

If a business finds that you been using their trademark, especially in the title or subtitle of a book, you'll receive a nasty letter from them telling you that you violated their trademark you need to take it down immediately. If you don't comply, those companies may take legal action and obtain damages if they can prove that there were any.

Chapter 8
Legal Concerns

Some companies, such as Microsoft, LinkedIn, and eBay, nicely provide whole pages on their websites that describe the rules for using their logos and trademarks. I found that these pages are generally very-well written and understandable, and they usually include a link to contact them if there any questions.

To find them, search on the web for their branding page. For example, to find LinkedIn's page, search for "linkedin branding guidelines". You can also find these pages by searching on the website itself, and, if all else fails, you can call or email them with your request.

Make sure you understand the rules for using those trademarks before you publish your book to avoid any complications. This is important to understand *before* you publish your book, as you cannot change the title of paperbacks and hardcovers. Thus, if you *do* need to change the title, you must retire your current version of the book and publish it again with the new title. This, by the way, causes you to lose all the reviews on the book.

LIBEL AND SLANDER

Defamation is "the act of making untrue statements about another which damages his/her reputation." (Legal Terms and Definitions n.d.).

Libel is "a written defamatory statement" and slander is a "spoken or oral defamatory statement" (Berg n.d.).

As you write your book, whether it's fiction or nonfiction, keep the definitions above in mind. To avoid legal action, you should avoid defaming any person, business or brand.

For example, if you wrote a book about someone having wild parties with many different people, and portrayed them in an unwholesome manner, they could have grounds to file a lawsuit. Including such things as a recognizable person who got drunk, took drugs, had an affair, committed criminal acts, and so forth could get you into trouble.

You can't just change the names to be protected. If the circumstances are recognizable, such that somebody reading the book would recognize who it was about, then they could successfully sue you for damages. And many have.

For example, if in your book, you stated that Miss Betsy committed adultery, and it was true and could be proven, then you haven't defamed her and there is no libel involved. Additionally, if Miss Betsy didn't care that anyone knew about her many affairs, and in fact told numerous people about them, then you'd probably also be safe writing about it.

On the other hand, if you wrote a book about the drug-taking lifestyle of a rock star and his band, and it wasn't true, then the rock star in the band would have grounds for a lawsuit.

In fiction, you could commit libel if the people and circumstances are recognizable, even if you don't name them explicitly. To be safe, you need to change more than just a few details. Change the appearances, location, habits, and the names so that the situation is unrecognizable to anyone else.

Chapter 8
Legal Concerns

Another interesting twist to the law is that you cannot defame somebody who is dead. In other words, the heirs cannot sue you for anything you say about their dead father or mother.

It's important to understand that libel and slander are not criminal actions – you cannot be put in jail for talking or writing bad things about another person, true or false. You can, however, be sued and, if you lose, be required pay damages.

If you're going to defame a person, product or company in writing, either make sure that what you write is true and you can prove it, or change the names and situations so that they are not recognizable. In the latter case, you'd be well-advised to run your book by a lawyer before publishing.

As a final note, you can be sued regardless of the merits of the suit. In that case, you could wind up spending thousands of dollars defending yourself even though the suit is dismissed. This is a good reason to ensure your writing is free from any possible issues.

CONCLUSIONS

You don't want people stealing your work and making money off what you have created, do you? Do onto others—and respect their copyrights.

I'm sure you wouldn't want someone writing untrue, malicious things about you, so don't write such things about others.

Respect the trademarks and service marks of businesses by following their rules (if any). In general, as long as you don't portray a trademark in a bad light and format it properly, you can include references in your book.

If you have any concerns about what you have written your book, you should consult your attorney.

Chapter 9
The Book Cover

The cover of your book is arguably the most important factor in converting lookers into buyers. In fact, the clear majority of people judge whether a book is worth buying based upon the cover.

As a rule, a book with a poorly-done cover won't sell well.

Your cover needs to communicate the contents of the book in an exciting and interesting way. The fonts, colors, graphics, and even the positions of each of the various components all go together to either attract readers, or push them away.

Additionally, different genres have different expectations about covers. For example, the style of a cover for romance book would be vastly different than that of a science fiction novel or nonfiction historical book. The expectations of the audiences of each of those genres is very different.

Chapter 9
The Book Cover

Professional Business Series #7

FOCUS ON LINKEDIN ™

Create a Personal Brand On LinkedIn to Make More Money, Generate Leads and Find Employment

Richard G Lowe Jr

It is critical that the title be large enough on the cover to be clearly read when the cover image is shown as a thumbnail, because this is what is displayed in listings of the book.

Designing a good cover is a science and an art, and generally, unless you have training as a graphics artist or designer, it's best to outsource the design and creation to someone skilled in that area.

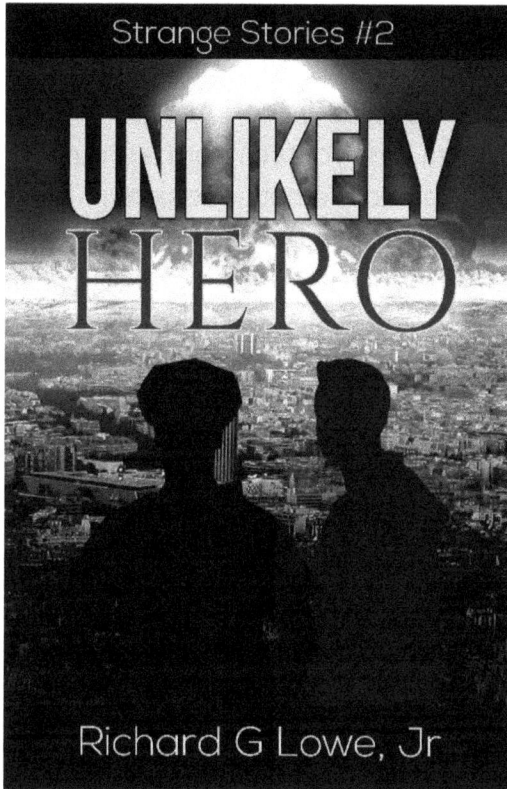

Fiverr.com is an excellent place to find people who can create book covers. Be sure to read their reviews and look over their samples to get a feel for their competence.

Make sure you have commercial licensing for the cover from the cover designer and *for any images that you use*. Many Fiverr.com gigs include a commercial license as an extra cost option, but I have found that by writing a quick email to the cover artist, they will create a custom gig that includes the commercial license at no charge.

Chapter 9
The Book Cover

It is important to understand that, even if the cover designer gives you commercial rights to the book cover, you **must** still ensure you can legally use the images. The best thing you can do is get the images yourself from a reputable stock photo site and supply them to the cover designer. This way you can make sure you have the necessary rights. Always read the fine print to ensure you have the rights to use those images commercially.

Don't randomly grab images from the web or elsewhere. Just because someone else steals an image and makes it public doesn't give you the right to do so.

Most gigs include several revisions, and you should ensure that they allow for at least two. Covers will often go through several revisions before you settle on one that pleases you.

On Fiverr.com, you can expect to pay $5 to $25 for a high-quality cover that works very well. A professional graphics artist, outside of Fiverr.com and similar sites, will charge anywhere from $100 to $500 for a high-quality cover.

Exercise: Go to Amazon.com and look at a dozen different books. Examine the covers closely. Do they want to make you look at or purchase the book?

MAKING COVERS YOURSELF

If you want to make your own book covers, Canva.com is a great place to start. Create an account and use their book cover template. They have a pre-made one for eBooks that works great. These covers are not as you'd get from a professional, but they are still good and you can't beat the price (free).

https://www.canva.com/create/book-covers/

If you can use a graphics editing program, you can purchase a set of cover templates. For example, one set of 25 covers can be obtained at a low cost from the link below.

http://smooth.li/kindlecovers
Note, this is an affiliate link. If you purchase the product I will receive a small commission.

You can edit these with either Adobe Photoshop, the free image-editing software called Gimp and other graphics programs that can read Adobe Photoshop files.

You can pick up a free copy of Gimp here:

https://www.gimp.org/

PAID COVER TEMPLATE SITE

The sites listed in this section contain options suitable for your average self-publisher. You can buy individual covers for between $75 and $200 – much less than hiring a professional cover designer.

You can get book covers from SelfPubBookCovers.com at a good rate. The site features pre-made covers and an interface allowing you to add your title, subtitle, author name and so on. Once you purchase a cover, the design is removed and is not sold again.

http://SelfPubBookCovers.com

Other book cover sites include:

- http://www.goonwrite.com/
- https://thebookcoverdesigner.com/
- https://www.creativindiecovers.com/ (They have an option for do-it-yourself covers for less than $100).
- https://www.coverdesignstudio.com/ (Do-it-yourself designed available as well as professional designers).

CONCLUSIONS

Designing a good book cover is one of the most important steps towards creating a book that sells well. If your book is not selling as well as you hoped, the first place to look is at the cover. Sometimes, even something minor, such as an incorrect font, the title being too small to read in a thumbnail, or graphic image that doesn't attract, can cause your book to be ignored by potential buyers.

The best alternative, given sufficient funding, is to engage the services of a professional book cover designer. However, these can run to a cost of thousands of dollars, which is out of the range of the budget of most self-published authors.

Fortunately, there are many other ways that you can get coverage created – from making them yourself in a graphics program to hiring someone on a site like Fiverr.com to using one of the premade cover services online.

There's much more to making a good cover than is covered in this short chapter. Entire books can be written about all the elements that go into creating a cover that looks good and causes people to want to buy the book.

Finally, don't be afraid to change your book cover if your book is not selling well. Get the opinions of other authors and readers, and, if appropriate, make changes. You might be surprised to find that your sales improve just from this small step.

Chapter 10
Metadata

Information about your book is called metadata. This includes the title, subtitle, author, other people who worked on your book (cover artist, editor, and so on), series, and ISBN number, among other things.

Before you publish your book, define and write down this information so you can easily enter it into KDP or CreateSpace.

The significant metadata is described in the following sections.

IMPRINT (PUBLISHER) NAME

If you're going to publish more than one book, or more than one edition of the same book, then consider defining an imprint (also known as a publishing company). This is just a name, and has nothing to do with a real-world publishing company or entity. You do not need to incorporate or file a DBA (Doing Business As) legal document to define a publisher[8].

There are two things you'll need to do: come up with a name, and purchase a block (preferably) of ISBN numbers.

---

[8] Although, of course, you can define a business if you want.

Chapter 10
Metadata

The name you choose should reinforce your brand – which is the image you are trying to portray to the outside world – and be consistent across all your books.

Some authors use the imprint name as another way to enter keywords, so it is different for all their books. While not forbidden, this violates the purpose of the publisher name, which is to identify your publishing company.

For example, if you are publishing coloring books you might define an imprint of "Ron's Coloring Books" or if you are an artist you could use "Zen Art". The name is entirely up to you. Just make sure it's not a domain name, a trademark or the name of another book.

If you want to use a publisher name or imprint, you will need to purchase and assign ISBN numbers.

Do not use the ISBN numbers, either free or for a fee, provided by CreateSpace, Lulu, or other publishing company. You must use ISBN numbers that you purchase and assign to get the full benefit of using your own imprint.

The imprint name shows up on your book page in the *Product Details* section, as in the example below ("The Writing King").

If you don't include one when you publish the book, it will show up as something like "Amazon Digital Services LLC".

Product Details

Series: Earn Money from Your Home
Paperback: 132 pages
Publisher: The Writing King (August 4 2016)
Language: English
ISBN-10: 1943517363
ISBN-13: 978-1943517367
Product Dimensions: 6 x 0 3 x 9 inches
Shipping Weight: 1 6 ounces (View shipping rates and policies)
Average Customer Review: ★★★★★ (25 customer reviews)
Amazon Best Sellers Rank: #93 948 in Books (See Top 100 in Books)
     #13 in Books > Computers & Technology > Internet & Social Media > eBay
     #92 in Books > Business & Money > Small Business & Entrepreneurship > Home Based

In addition, you should include the imprint name on the title page of each edition of your books. For eBooks, I include a link below the title to my publisher website so that my readers can visit to look at my other books and projects.

Exercise: Make a list of possible Imprint Names that promote the brand and image you want to portray. Look over the list and keep adding to it until you find a name that works for you.

ISBN NUMBER

An ISBN, or International Standard Book Number, is commonly assigned to each edition and variation of a book. They are used by bookstores, libraries, and so forth to identify each specific title and edition.

The ISBN number was not optional back in the days of traditional publishing and bookselling. If a book didn't have an ISBN number, it would not be on the shelves of bookstores and libraries. Authors normally didn't have to deal with assigning them because this was done by publishers. With self-publishing, authors who write and publish their own books must take responsibility for deciding whether to use ISBN numbers, and then purchasing them if needed.

There is some debate as to whether ISBN numbers are even necessary anymore, at least with electronic books such as those for the Kindle or the Nook. In fact, the ISBN number is optional when publishing a book for Kindle because Amazon uses an internal number, called an ASIN, to identify your book.

For paperbacks, Amazon, under the CreateSpace umbrella, will give you a free ISBN number if you choose. This shows your book as being published by Amazon, rather than by you.

If you decide to get your own ISBN numbers, you'll need to head on over to Bowker.com and purchase them[9]. You can purchase just one, which is very expensive, a block of ten, or a block of one hundred, which is the best deal commonly used by self-publishers.

http://Bowker.com

If you publish more than one version of your book, for example an eBook (optionally), a paperback, and hardcover, then you'll need one ISBN number for each one. Also, if you republish the book as a new edition, then you must get a new ISBN number for it as well.

---

[9] Bowker is the source of all ISBN numbers in the United States. For other countries, you'll need to find who provides the numbers.

As you can see, if you publish a lot of books you could wind up going through quite a few ISBN numbers.

You have the option of purchasing ISBN numbers through your publisher, for example CreateSpace, but if you're going to do that you may as well purchase your own directly from Bowker.com.

The website for Bowker.com can be a little intimidating to navigate. However, once you have gone through it once or twice, you'll find that becomes friendlier. If you need help, Bowker has a customer service number at the top of their website, and they'll be happy to guide you through the process and explain what everything means.

There are several reasons why you may want or need to use your own ISBN numbers.

- If you want to sell your book to libraries or bookstores, you must use ISBN numbers.
- An ISBN number along with a publisher name adds a certain amount of credibility to your publishing business. This raises you from being "merely" a self-publisher to being an honest to God publisher.
- If you want to sell your book on other retailers, such as iBook, you will need ISBN numbers.
- If you want your eBook to rank on Google, you'll need ISBN numbers to list the book in Bowker's *Books in Print* database.
- Some countries require ISBN numbers.

Chapter 10
Metadata

Exercise: Visit the Bowker website, create an account if you don't already have one, and read through the documentation.

PCN NUMBER

For your paperback and hardcover versions, you should make the effort to acquire a PCN number. These numbers are what the United States Library of Congress uses to identify books, and the entire US library system follows their lead.

In the United States, if you want your book to be acquired by libraries, you need to get a PCN number.

PCN numbers are free of charge, except that you will need to send a copy of the book to the Library of Congress once it is published.

Before submitting books to the PCN system, you'll need to get an ISBN number for each one at Bowker.com, as described in the previous section. You can't use ISBN numbers that are provided by CreateSpace or other platforms.

http://www.bowker.com/

The PCN program is intended for book publishers and not individual authors. However, all you need to do to be a publisher is to define an imprint name, maintain an office in the United States and be able answer questions about your books from that office.

To create an account, click the link below

https://www.loc.gov/publish/pcn/

And click on the link titled "Open an Account", read each of the sections that are linked from this page, then click on "Application to Participate" and fill out the form.

Once you've been accepted into the program, which occurs quickly, each time you want to publish a book, click the link below at least a week in advance of your publication date and fill in the information.

http://smooth.li/pcn

Once you've entered all the information into the form, it will be submitted, and generally within anywhere from a day to week you'll receive back your Library of Congress number. This needs to be recorded in two places.

- On the copyright page of your book
- In the *Library of Congress Control Number* field of the ISBN database entry for your book on Bowker.com. This is on the first page of the listing.

KEYWORDS

Before you create your title, subtitle, description, or any other metadata, stop and come up with your keywords. Once you have those keywords defined, sprinkle them through your description, title, and subtitle.

Come up with a string of keywords that is about 400 characters long, each separated by a space. These don't need to be in any particular order. Don't include common words (stop words) such as "to", "the", "and" and so forth, and don't worry about plurals.

The following sentence from the KDP help text sums up nicely how you should be entering keywords:

> *Quotation marks in search terms: Single words work better than phrases—and specific words work better than general words. If you enter "complex suspenseful whodunit," only people who type all of those words will find your book. You'll get better results if you enter this: complex suspenseful whodunit.* **_Customers can search on any of those words and find your book._**

As you can see, it clearly states that any words that are included in your keyword fields can be used to search for your book. This implies that Amazon search does not use key phrases – it only uses keywords.

Review the document in the link below which describes Amazon's rules for keywords thoroughly. Make sure you understand all their restrictions and recommendations.

http://smooth.li/kdpkey

For example, let's say your book is about the history of television. You could come up with a string of words about the subjects you discuss in your book.

> television American culture biography production handbook history platinum age criticism writing radio announcing TV antenna advertising actor actress

Your book can be discovered via searches on any of the keywords listed above. Simply enter this string of words into the keyword field in KDP. Note the newer version of KDP includes seven fields, so just split this up among each of them.

You can use the Bing Keyword Research Tool [10] to come up with words to use as keywords.

http://smooth.li/bingkey

You'll need to create a Microsoft account to use this tool, which is intended to be used to find keywords to purchase for Bing advertisements. However, you can use it just to find keywords without purchasing anything.

Sprinkle your keywords – and phrases – in your title, subtitle and description. Put your most important words and phrases near the front of these three fields.

To make this easy, create an account on booksprout.com:

https://booksproutapp.com/

This website has a keyword tool which can help you come up with strings of keywords to use for your book. When you're done, just copy them into the keyword fields in KDP and CreateSpace.

Exercise: Practice using the Bing Keyword Research Tool and Book Sprout to find keywords for your book or topic.

---

[10] The Google Keyword Planner is no longer as useful as it was in the past because the results that are returned are generalized unless you've purchased Google ads.

Chapter 10
Metadata

TITLE

A well-designed title can make the difference between a book that earns money and a book that sells poorly.

There are two audiences for your book title.

- People who might want to purchase your book.
- The indexing system of Amazon or your publishing company (and other search engines such as Google and Bing).

Your title and, to a lesser extent, subtitle, should consider both audiences.

The title must be understandable by human beings and often needs to appeal to some emotion such as fear, anger, joy, greed, love or even hate. A good title is memorable, stands out from the competition, and communicates the subject matter of the fiction or nonfiction contents.

At the same time, Amazon and search engines are looking for keywords and phrases to aid in indexing that book, so that people may find it when they're searching for information on a topic.

There are whole books and courses that teach how to create a good title, and there are many tools available which will construct a title out of keywords and phrases.

Some of the restrictions in a title are:

- As discussed in the section *Using Trademarks in the Title*, ensure you understand the legalities of using a trademark in the title of your book before you publish it.

- It is tempting to create a long, keywords stuffed title, and it is best to avoid this temptation. Keep it between 30 and 80 characters. You want long enough to communicate the meaning but not so long that it appears to be spammy.

- Your title must appear exactly as written on the cover image of your book. Amazon, and probably other platforms as well, review your title and cover at the point at which you publish to ensure this is true.

- You can change the title on a Kindle eBook any time you want before and after you publish[11]. However, on a paperback, Amazon does not allow the title to be changed after the book has been published and made live. The titles of hardcover versions may not be changed either.

Amazon tends to prioritize keywords and phrases within the title higher than anything else in your book description, subtitle, keywords, and elsewhere. In addition, **keywords and phrases that are closer to the front of the title are given priority** over those near the end. For example, the words "make money" in the title "Make Money on Internet" are given more weight than in "Insider Tips on How to Make Money on the Internet".

---

[11] Bowker states that once you've published a book with an ISBN number, the title, subtitle, author, series and so forth should not be changed, even for eBooks. However, the website will allow you to make changes, but the best practice is not to change your title and other metadata after publication.

Chapter 10
Metadata

Don't include advertising and promotions as part of your title (or subtitle) — for example, "free" or "reduced price". Don't reference other titles or authors, use the word best-selling or any other ranking, and only use a trademarked word when you have permission. These guidelines are all discussed thoroughly in the Amazon document on guidelines:

http://smooth.li/metadata

A well-written title with good keywords and phrases will get you more potential buyers than a poorly-written title simply because of the way Amazon, and other search engines as well, creates its index.

If you are having trouble coming up with a good title, this free title generator can help:

http://smooth.li/freetitles

Exercise: Go to the free title generator page (above) and experiment with creating titles.

SUBTITLE

The subtitle is intended to communicate additional information about the content of your book. As with the title, avoid keyword stuffing and create a subtitle that is valuable to people as well as to Amazon and search engine indexing.

The keywords and key phrases within the subtitle don't carry as much weight as the title, but they are still used by Amazon to index the book.

Per Amazon's help page, the book title plus the subtitle together must be less than two hundred characters long.

SERIES

Consider creating one or more book series. By doing this, you tell your readers that you'll be coming out with additional titles on that subject and you can build promotional campaigns around that fact.

That's why in fiction you will commonly see trilogies or even longer series of books. Fans of those books get interested in the storyline and characters and want to read more. Authors who are on the ball and want to make more income can take advantage of this and create series in the same universe as the first book.

This also works well for nonfiction in that you can create a series of books about business, home repair, finance, or any number of other topics. This allows you to create books that tie together and work to sell each other.

DESCRIPTION

It's a shame to spend money and effort to get people to your Amazon Book Page, only to turn them away with a poorly-written book description.

Next to the cover and title, your book description is your most important selling tool. You have 4,000 characters, which is several pages, to entice lookers into buyers.

Chapter 10
Metadata

Your first sentence is the most important. Use it to grab your reader and pull them into the rest of the description. Start off with a shocking statement or question.

In the first few paragraphs, cater to emotions – anger, fear, hate, terror, love and joy are much more powerful than facts and reasoning. For non-fiction, show you understand their plight and are sympathetic – in fact, the book has the answers. For fiction, hint at a dark secret or a terror or something to that effect.

Once you've got the emotions stirred up, tell them a little bit about what's in your book. Then go right back and stir up some emotions.

For non-fiction, include a bulleted list of some of the things they will learn. This helps with keywords (Amazon will use those in its search index) and informs your reader. Put this list near the bottom of your description – the emotions are more important.

Use HTML tags to format your description. The more useful ones are described below.

- <b> means to bold the text: <b>This is bolded</b>
-
 means insert a line break: Here's a line

- <h1> define a header: <h1>Header goes here</h1>
- <h2> to <h6> work the same as H1
- <hr> inserts a horizontal line: <hr>
- <i> is italics: <i>italicize this</i>
- <li> identifies a line in a bulleted or numbered list (see examples below)

- <p> defines a paragraph: <p>text goes here</p>
- <u> formats as underlined: <u>underline this</u>

An example of a bulleted list:

```
<ul>
     <li>Line 1</li>
     <li>Line 2</li>
</ul>
```

And a numbered list:

```
<ol>
     <li>List 1</li>
     <li>List 2</li>
</ol>
```

A complete list of HTML tags is described on the following page:

http://smooth.li/kdphtml

Use HTML to format your description so that it stands out from all the others on Amazon. Use <h1> for your primary headings, create a bulleted list for your benefits and such, and use <b> and <i> to emphasize keywords and important points.

If you want to find out more about how to create a book description that sells, check out the product Hypnotic Book Descriptions.

Chapter 10
Metadata

CATEGORIES

Imagine a bookstore or library with books randomly placed on shelves anywhere in the establishment with no order. Would this make it difficult to find the books that you want?

KDP and CreateSpace use an industry-standard system called BISAC codes, which categorize books into various subjects. One way to think of it is that these codes define the bookshelves for your books.

The following website describes BISAC codes.

http://smooth.li/bisac

Amazon uses these code as a base, and translates them into its own structure of organization. This can make it confusing to find the right code for your book, since the category that you found on Amazon may not match a BISAC code.

For your Kindle books on KDP you can choose two codes and on CreateSpace you can choose one.

A good way to determine the appropriate categories is to look at those used by similar books.

Some sample categories from one of my coloring books is shown below.

Books > Arts & Photography > Drawing > Coloring Books for Grown-Ups
Books > Crafts, Hobbies & Home > Crafts & Hobbies

You'll find many books that have more than two categories, and you'll find other books that are in categories that don't exist in the BISAC structure.

You can send a message to Amazon to request a specific category using the contact link at the bottom of the KDP or CreateSpace website. You'll need the ASIN or ISBN number of the book to change.

For example:

> Please add my book 1237846 to the following category:
>
> Books > Arts & Photography > Graphic Design > Techniques > Use of Color

For KDP, to get into certain categories you must include specific keywords in your keyword fields.

For example, to get your book placed in the following category:

History>Americas>United States>Civil War>Campaigns & Battlefields>Antietam

You must include the keyword "antietam" in a keyword field.

Read the following page for information about categories. This page also includes links to pages which describe the specific keywords you must include in your keyword fields to get your books placed into certain special categories.

http://smooth.li/category

CONCLUSIONS

Spend the time to create the metadata for your book. This information is used by Amazon to create your Book Page, to help readers find your books, and as submissions to search engines and book indexes.

Decisions about your title, subtitle, series name, and ISBN number can dramatically affect your sales. A poorly thought-out title, for example, can make your book unfindable or unattractive to your readers.

Chapter 11
Parts of a Book

Several standards have been accepted by publishers over the years regarding what should be in the front and back of a book. The purpose of these standards is to give readers, publishers, bookstores, and libraries some consistency from book to book and to ensure that all necessary information is included and in a predictable location.

The standards for eBooks are slightly different than those for paperbacks and hardcovers. This puts more of the actual book at the front of eBooks where it can be seen in the "look inside" feature available on Amazon and other publishers. Platforms such as Amazon take the first 10% or so of your book and make it available on the Book Page so that readers can review a chapter or two to get an idea of what the book is about before they make a purchase.

If you fill up the look inside preview with copyright, series, and other materials, readers will not be able to preview what your book is about and you are less likely to make a sale.

Because of this, it is acceptable to either move some of the front material to the back (such as a list of an author's other books, traditionally part of the front material) or skip including it entirely.

The title page and copyright page should always be in the front of eBooks.

Chapter 11
Parts of a Book

Paperbacks and hardcovers are typically printed on the front and back of each page. The preface, introduction, table of contents, and each chapter should begin on an odd numbered page, and some other information such as the copyright and series pages are designed to begin on in even page.

FRONT MATTER

In the front, there are typically several pages set aside that identifies the contents, subject and other information about the book.

ENDORSEMENTS PAGE

If you get endorsements for your book in advance of publication you can include them on a page in front of everything. Endorsements are especially valuable from known influencers and leaders in your target audience. This is always on the odd page and the back (even page) should be blank.

An endorsements page is optional in the eBook version.

HALF TITLE PAGE

The half title page contains only your book title and author name, centered and in a large font, placed about a third of the way down the page. You can also include the subtitle, although this is not standard, if you want. This page is typically not included in eBooks.

FRONTISPIECE

This is an illustration on the back of the half title page. For coloring, puzzle and comic books, include one of the drawings from inside the book so it will show up in the "Look Inside" feature on the Amazon book page.

You can include either a Frontispiece or a Series page but generally not both.

This is typically not included in eBooks.

As a note, on my coloring books, I include a sample or two on the Frontispiece so that it shows up on the "Look Inside" for the book.

THE SERIES PAGE OR OTHER BOOKS PAGE

This section appears on the back of the half title page and contains a list of previously published books. Some authors list them from most recent to oldest, and others list by series. This is not included on eBooks.

If you do want to include a list of your other titles and series in an eBook, add it to the *Back Matter* instead of the *Front Matter*.

THE TITLE PAGE

The title page is always on the odd side, and includes the book title, subtitle, author, and publisher name.

THE COPYRIGHT PAGE

See Chapter 13 for information on the Copyright Page.

DEDICATION

Optionally, a few words or sentences dedicating the book to someone or an organization. This takes up a full odd numbered page. The back page should be blank.

Chapter 11
Parts of a Book

FORWARD

An introduction is a short essay, usually written by someone else, to help promote or introduce the book. It begins on an odd page, and the numbering is typically in lower-case Roman numerals beginning with "i".

PREFACE

This is the introduction written by the author to explain how the book came about. You can include a personal anecdote or story to give the reader some context for the book. It begins on an odd page number.

ACKNOWLEDGEMENTS

Write as much as you want to acknowledge anyone who helped you create the book. Some authors get very specific and thank everyone who even remotely helped, others just thank a few friends, and many leave this section off entirely. This begins on an odd page.

TABLE OF CONTENTS

The table of contents can be automatically generated based upon header styles by Microsoft Word and other word processers. In Word, these are Heading 1, Heading 2 and so on. If you use the built-in styles for headings, you can generate your table of contents automatically.

For paperbacks and hardcovers, the page numbers are included in the table of contents. For eBooks, page numbers are not included. Instead, each link of the contents should be a clickable link to the appropriate page in the book.

Important note: Sometimes you'll find table of contents placed at the end of the book in eBooks. Amazon frowns upon this practice and prefers this be placed at the front.

Important note: if you're also planning to publish on Smashwords, you cannot use the table of contents generated by Word. You must use a hyperlinked list. To do this, insert a bookmark at the start of each section you want to include in the table of contents. When that is done, link each line in the table of contents to the appropriate bookmark. This is fully described on the Smashwords website.

LIST OF ILLUSTRATIONS

Optionally, list any illustrations or photos included in your book.

LIST OF TABLES

Optionally, list any tables included in the book.

INTRODUCTION

The introduction serves to summarize or present the subject of the book. This can be as short or as long as you want, and begins on an odd page.

THE BACK OF THE BOOK

There are a lot of sections that you could put at the back of the book. Traditionally, nonfiction books include an index, an author biography (about the author), list of references if applicable, and possibly a glossary if there are technical terms.

However, there is no reason why you can't include more (or even less) if you want. In the modern world of self-publishing, whether digital or print on demand, there is little concern about space or the cost of these extra pages[12]. Don't go overboard, but feel free to include extra materials if you see fit.

Take advantage of the space to give your reader more information, to tell them about yourself, help them find things in the book or give them definitions, and advertise your other books and services.

REFERENCES
For nonfiction works, include a list of any books or other materials that you believe will help your readers. This is an optional section.

GLOSSARY
Optionally, include a list of words and definitions to help your readers when they run into technical or obscure language. Note: you cannot just copy definitions from the dictionary – that's copyright infringement. Paraphrase the definitions in your own words.

END NOTES
If you have any citations in your nonfiction book, list them here.

---

[12] There is a cost-per-page for paperbacks; the more pages in the book, the higher the price you will need to charge. For Kindle, you are charged to send the book to the Kindle, but unless you have a lot of large images, this cost is very low.

You can read about how to use citations here:

http://smooth.li/cite

Citing your sources is considered good form. Not doing so is plagiarism. Always cite your sources.

INDEX

> *"Indexing work is not recommended to those who lack an orderly mind and a capacity for taking pains. A good index is a minor work of art but it is also the product of clear thought and meticulous care."* —**Peter Farrell, How to Make Money from Home**

Most eBooks don't include indexes since the contents can be searched directly from the Kindle or other eBook reader. However, if that book also appears in paperback or hardcover, then you may want to consider including an index in those editions.

Creating an index is not as easy as you would think. It's not just a matter of finding every occurrence of certain words or keywords, marking them in your word processor, and listing them at a table in the back of the book. This creates a relatively useless hodgepodge of chaos that is difficult to use and doesn't serve the purpose of an index.

The reason an index exists is to give your readers the ability to find the important passages related to a specific keyword or phrase directly, without having to read the rest of the book.

Chapter 11
Parts of a Book

Definitions or vital information may be bolded in the index, and titles of books may be italicized. You can also specify a page number or range of page numbers.

Thus, you don't want to mark every single occurrence of a keyword. Instead, pick out the references that are important to your readers; the ones that give them an answer to whatever question is on their mind at that point in time.

Believe it or not, there is an entire writing specialty devoted to creating indexes. In fact, there is an Association that helps those people who specialize in this field.

http://www.asindexing.org/

Generally, short nonfiction paperback or hardbound books don't require indexes. However, in a longer work you may want to consider creating one.

Your word processor should include the ability to mark entries for the index and then use that to create the actual index itself. For example, the index capabilities of Microsoft Word are excellent and easy to use.

If you decide to create an index for your book, be sure to do it right. Read through some of the resources listed on asindexing.org before you start or, if you have the budget, hire someone to do it for you.

ABOUT THE AUTHOR
You should always include an *About the Author* section in the back of your book. This can be as short or long as you want, but generally one to three pages is more than enough.

The purpose of this is to present a biography of yourself, or in the case of a pen name, of a made-up person. This is your opportunity for you to build your brand and add to your credibility.

Generally, this section is written in the third person as if someone was talking about you. However, sometimes first-person works just fine, especially if a little bit of humor is injected.

This is a great place for you to talk about your life as an author, why you started writing, your background, and anything else that you feel would be of interest to your readers.

Always include a picture, generally a headshot, to give your readers an idea of who you are. Of course, if you're writing under a pen name, that may be more difficult. Some authors may use a drawing and others may skip the picture entirely.

I recommend that you include a link to your website, LinkedIn and Facebook profiles (if you have them), and your Twitter name. If you want to be contacted via email, also include your email address.

Remember this is not a sales page, and you should not use this opportunity to sell products or services or other books that you written.

OTHER BOOKS AND SERVICES
At the tail end of every book that I've written under my own name, I include a list of other books that I've written, as well as a page describing the services that I provide in all the various websites that I support.

Chapter 11
Parts of a Book

This gives my readers the opportunity to find all my other offerings if they so desire. This section is the same in every book, and I keep it to a maximum of one page long and insure it is always on an odd page.

Chapter 12
The Copyright Page

THE COPYRIGHT PAGE

The copyright information is always on the back of the title page where it can be easily found by readers, publishers, libraries and bookstores.

There is a lot of information contained on this single page, and it can be very intimidating because it's typically printed in small type and contains formidable legal words.

It's best to keep your copyright page as short as you can while still containing all the necessary information. Except in rare circumstances, it should not be over one page in length.

In the rest of this section, we're only going to go over those parts of the copyright page pertinent to self-publishing. Traditionally published books include other information either not needed or unavailable for self-published works.

COPYRIGHT NOTICE

All copyright pages require the copyright notice. This short line defines exactly who owns the copyright on the book.

- Begin with a copyright symbol ©, the word "Copyright" or both. The use of (c) should be avoided as it may not stand up in court.
- The year the work was published for the first time.

229

- The name of the owner of the copyright, which can be a pen name.

Note that your work is copyrighted (at least in the United States) from the moment it was created and you do not need to file with the copyright office. However, registering your work with the copyright office is valuable if you need to prove in court that you own the rights to the work.

RIGHTS

Next, include a paragraph or more describing the rights to you allow and disallow for your work. Typically, this includes the words "All rights reserved" followed by a few sentences describing how the work may or may not be used.

The rest of the legalese depends upon your requirements and what kind of protections you believe you need.

> *Although every precaution has been taken to verify the accuracy of the information contained herein, the author and publisher assume no responsibility for any errors or omissions. No liability is assumed for damages that may result from the use of information contained within.*

If you use any trademarks within your book that don't belong to you, it's wise to include a paragraph stating that you're using them in editorial fashion and don't intend to infringe.

> *Trademarked names appear throughout this book. Rather than use a trademark symbol with every occurrence of a trademarked name, names are used in an editorial fashion, with no intention of infringement of the respective owner's trademark.*

Depending upon your needs, the legalese can be much longer or shorter.

Chapter 12
The Copyright Page

LIBRARY OF CONGRESS NUMBER

If you went to the trouble of getting an <u>LOCC number</u>, then include that in your copyright page.

> *Library of Congress Control Number: 2016921009*

ISBN

Include the ISBN number of your book, if you have one. If you have multiple versions, such as an eBook, paperback and hardcover, list the ISBN numbers of each edition.

I like to include the ASIN number of the eBook version, which identifies it in the Amazon database. Note if you include the ASIN number, you will need to publish the eBook, get the ASIN number that was assigned upon publication, insert it into your copyright page, and then republish the eBook with the updated information.

> *ASIN: B01H9BSCAW*
> *ISBN: 978-1-943517-98-5 (Hardcover)*
> *ISBN: 978-1-943517-97-8 (Paperback)*
> *ISBN: 978-1-943517-96-1 (eBook)*

Do not include words such as Amazon, Kindle, or the equivalent from other publishers. If you ever want to publish your book on platforms such as iBook, which is the Apple bookstore, your book will be rejected if you include competitor names on the copyright page or elsewhere in the text.

Thus, if you have an ISBN for the Barnes & Noble Nook tablet and an ISBN for your Kindle version, simply list them both as eBooks without specifying the tablet type.

CONTRIBUTORS

It is good form to include a list of those who contributed to the book in the final section of your copyright page. This includes book designers, proofreaders, editors, cover designers, indexers, and anyone else that helped you with any part of your book.

CONCLUSIONS

Once you've defined one copyright page, you can use it as a template for all your other books.

The copyright page is vital, as it communicates the legalities associated with your book. Additionally, it contains other information in a standard location that is available to libraries, bookstores and indexes.

Chapter 13
Publishing

Once you written your book, it's time to publish it to Amazon and possibly other publishers as well. You can choose to publish in one, several or all the following:

- Kindle eBook
- Paperback
- Hardcover
- Audiobook

Each of these formats are discussed in this chapter as well as the various options relative to each that available to you.

Before you can publish anywhere, you need to write and format a book, create a cover (depending on the format you may need a back cover as well), assign an ISBN number (optional in some cases), and define the book's metadata.

For at least the first few times you publish, you'll probably find it to be a frustrating and challenging experience. There's a lot to learn, and quite a bit of specialized terminology which applies to the publishing and printing industry. However, once you get used to the process, it will become easier and less stressful.

On Amazon, there is no charge for publishing to paperback or Kindle. For audiobooks through ACX (owned by Amazon), you have the option of hiring a producer for a 50% cut of the royalties, making the production free of charge, or you can pay an actor and get 100% of the royalties. IngramSpark charges for publishing under normal conditions, but often sends out coupons to let you publish free of charge[13].

FOCUS ON AMAZON

In this book, we are primarily concerned with publishing on Amazon because it's by far the largest market for self-published books.

One of the great things about self-publishing is that you have a lot more options than you do if you go with a traditional publisher. You get to choose things such as the price of the book, its dimensions (width and height), whether it's black-and-white or color, and even more importantly, its format (eBook, paperback, hardcover and so on).

Although your sales opportunities are generally by far the greatest with Amazon, there are several other publishers that you can choose for your book. These include Lulu, IngramSpark, iBook, Kobo and Barnes & Noble, to name a few. Each of these has their advantages and disadvantages, and some of them can sell their books through Amazon.

KDP SELECT

When you publish your book on Kindle using KDP, you have the option of placing your book into KDP Select. This gives you some additional royalty and promotional opportunities.

---

[13] Subscribe to IngramSpark's email list to receive notifications of coupons that they publish.

Since the terms are subject to change, you should review the information on the following page:

http://smooth.li/kdpselect

Currently, the benefits include:

- If an Amazon customer joins Kindle Unlimited, they can read Kindle eBooks free of charge. If you opt into KDP Select, your book can be read free, and you receive a share of the KDP Select Global Fund.
- You earn 70% royalties for sales in Japan, India, Brazil and Mexico.
- Every 90 days, you can use either a countdown deal or a free promotion for about a week if you want. The countdown deal shows a countdown clock next to the price.
- You can enter your books into Kindle Lending Library. Each time your book is lent you get money added to your part of the KDP Select Global Fund.

On the downside, by opting into KDP Select, your book may not be electronically distributed in any other form at any price, including free of charge. This means you cannot sell an electronic version from your blog, website, or other eBook formats.

Should you enroll your books into Kindle Select? The benefits are substantial – I've seen a definite increase in my income because of the program.

One reason NOT to include your book in the program is if you want to sell it on a platform such as Smashwords,

Chapter 13
Publishing

Draft2Digital, iBook, or even directly as a download from your blog.

FORMATS

If you decide you want to stick with Amazon as your book publisher, you have three options: Kindle, paperback and audiobook. Considering that you can publish to each for no cost, you'd be wise to publish your books in all three. Of course, coloring books, puzzle books, and other consumables can't be published as audiobooks or on the Kindle.

PAPERBACK
Paperbacks are published using Createspace.com. These are actual physical books which are printed on demand. This means that they are created immediately after a customer orders. There is no upfront charge for using CreateSpace — but you'll split the profits with them if the book sells.

KINDLE
Kindle is an electronic book format that works on Amazon proprietary Kindle eReaders (they also provide applications for most other devices). Books published in this format cannot include niceties such as numbered lists, positioned graphics, and many of the other things that you can use in paperbacks to make your books more attractive. These electronic books are published using kdp.com.

I've written a book which goes into detail about self-publishing on Kindle called How to Publish on Kindle. This book goes through each step of the process from beginning to end.

http://mybooks.space/pubkindle

AUDIOBOOK

Audiobooks are recordings of your book. You can choose to record these yourself or use acx.com (owned by Amazon) to hire someone to do it for you. In this case, you have the option of choosing a 50/50 royalty split with the actor or paying them directly and taking 100% of the royalties.

http://www.acx.com

HARDCOVER

If you want to publish a hardcover version of your book, then you must use the services of Ingramspark.com or Lulu.com. I went to the trouble of creating hardcover copies of all my nonfiction books and was surprised that they sell relatively well. I took advantage of a coupon from IngramSpark so the publishing was free. Both Lulu and IngramSpark sell books on Amazon and other distributors.

WHICH FORMAT?

For every non-consumable book that you publish, you should create at a minimum a Kindle eBook, a paperback and an audiobook version. Each one of these appeals to a different audience, and you will find that you'll receive sales spread over all three types of books.

Not publishing in all three formats for books is leaving money on the table. Since there is no cost involved in creating any of them, except for time, then I recommend that you go through the trouble to do it.

You can also create a hardcover on IngramSpark which will be sold on Amazon. Ingram charges a small fee – take advantage of their regularly released coupons.

DISTRIBUTION

On CreateSpace you'll see that there are six channels, three of them are internal to Amazon and three of them that are external - bookstores, libraries and so forth. When you define your paperback, you get to choose which channels you want to use to distribute your book.

You should always select, unless you have good reasons to do otherwise, the internal channels: Amazon.com, Amazon Europe, and CreateSpace eStore. This will make your paperback available to the widest possible audience using Amazon.com and its affiliates.

If you want to use Amazon to distribute to other channels such as bookstores and libraries, select the external channels – you may as well select all that you can.

However, many bookstores won't carry books sold through these channels because CreateSpace does not offer steep discounts or allow returns.

If you want bookstores to order your books and if you use your own ISBN numbers, then don't select any of the expanded distribution channels. Instead, send an email and tell them to transfer the ISBN number over to IngramSpark for expanded distribution.

To: info@createspace.com

Please transfer ISBN xxxxxxxxx from expanded distribution ONLY to IngramSpark. Please notify me once the transfer is complete.

Where xxxxxxxxx is the ISBN number that you want to move.

While you're waiting for response, if you haven't already created an account on IngramSpark, then go ahead and do so.

After a couple of business days, CreateSpace will get back to you and tell you that the ISBN numbers have been moved. Next, contact IngramSpark via email and tell them that you want to transfer those ISBN numbers into your account.

To: ingramsparksupport@ingramcontent.com

Can you please transfer the following titles into my account? My account number is yyyyyyy and the ISBN number is xxxxxxxxx. Please set these as NO RETURNS.

Where yyyyyyy is your IngramSpark account number and xxxxxxxxx is the ISBN number.

They will ask you to fill out a Title Transfer Addendum, and will send a copy to you. Print the form, fill it out, scan it to PDF format, and reply to their email with that form as an attachment.

After a few days, you'll get an email from them saying the task has been completed. At that point, your books will show up in your IngramSpark account, and they will also be present in your CreateSpace account. IngramSpark will now do the expanded distribution, and CreateSpace will distribute to Amazon.

Go into your IngramSpark account and make sure your prices and other information are correct.

One of the advantages of using this method instead of creating a paperback on both IngramSpark and CreateSpace, is that this only uses one ISBN number.

Thanks to Melinda Clayton for this tip from a guest post in Indies Unlimited (Clayton 2016).

RETURNS

When you publish paperbacks or hardcovers on IngramSpark, never allow returns. Before you publish, make sure the option to allow returns is set to NO, and double-check it again.

This is important, because if set to YES, bookstores have the option to return books that don't sell. IngramSpark will refund that money to them from your account balance, and you'll get mailed the books, which are often in terrible, unusable condition.

If you accidently set this option to YES then change it to NO, returns will be allowed for 6 months.

In theory, allowing returns makes it more likely that bookstores will purchase your books, since they don't have the risk associated with not selling. As a small publisher, you shouldn't take on that risk yourself.

Save yourself the time and hassle by not allowing returns.

OTHER ELECTRONIC FORMATS

In addition to Kindle, there are several other electronic formats to choose from. However, eBooks enrolled in KDP Select can't be published in any of these other formats because of the terms and conditions of that program.

If your book is not enrolled in KDP Select, two good choices for publishing are the iBook and the Nook. iBook is Apple's platform for electronic books, and the Nook is supported by Barnes & Noble.

You can also publish your book in PDF format. PDF stands for Portable Document Format and it was created by Adobe to allow documents to be viewed on any platform including Windows, Apple, Linux, tablets and elsewhere.

PDF is valuable for creating a version of your book that is downloadable from your blog or elsewhere. I commonly use it to give away the first or second chapter of a book for free as a teaser. Microsoft Word has a "save to PDF" option or you can use any number of PDF conversion tools available on the web.

Chapter 13
Publishing

SMASHWORDS AND DRAFT2DIGITAL

You can manually submit your book in the proper format to all the various publishers, and there are quite a few of them, or you could use one of the publishing aggregators such as Smashwords and Draft2Digital.

These companies accept your document in Word or PDF format, validate it, convert it, and send it off to each publisher (excluding Amazon) for you. They pay you royalties based upon sales, and have a reporting system seeking keep track of how things are doing.

If you don't have an Apple computer system, using aggregator such as this is the easiest way to get your book published in iBook format. Otherwise, you'll have to get access to an Apple system, because the software doesn't run on Windows.

The formatting for the books you submit to these two companies, and others, can be a little tricky. Their documentation is extensive and quite long, and your best option is to read all the way through and make sure you understand what you need to do before you try to submit anything to them.

CONCLUSIONS

At first, publishing can seem like a difficult and confusing process. There are many options and words unique to the publishing industry, and the learning curve can be steep.

Take your time, read the tutorials and help files for each format, and you'll get through it just fine. Once you've published a few books, the entire process becomes second nature.

Chapter 14
Networking

> *Social media is an amazing tool, but it's really the face-to-face interaction that makes a long-term impact.* —**Felicia Day**

One of the most important things that you can do to advance your writing career is to build a network of other writers, publishers, promoters, and readers. This was one of the most difficult things for me, since I tend to be a little introverted and prefer writing in front of a keyboard over being in a group of people at an event.

Regardless, it is vital that all self-published authors find people in their area and on the Internet who can both help them and whom they can help.

Networking works both ways — in fact, the best way to network is to be willing to give without receiving any benefit. This is easier than it sounds.

For example, I have many contacts with outsourcers who can help with proofreading, book covers, promotion, formatting and so forth. If someone in my network approaches me for help creating a book cover, I can refer them to one of several book cover creators.

The idea is to be willing to help people, and that help doesn't necessarily need to come from yourself. Once you become known as someone who has the contacts for anything, you'll be amazed at how quickly a group forms around you.

Chapter 14
Networking

You can network just about anywhere. In your local area, check out local writing groups, associations, libraries, and even networking groups or your Chamber of Commerce. On the Internet, join writing groups on Facebook, LinkedIn, and other social media and search out and join writing associations.

BUILD A NETWORK

It is very difficult to make a living in a vacuum. As with any profession, you need help from other people. Sure, you can write that book all by yourself with no help from anyone — but there are only so many hours in the day, and doing all the things that you need to do to be successful as a professional writer may take more time than you have.

You have the option of outsourcing, which means to pay other people to do work for you. It's relatively easy to find people on the web who will do high quality jobs for you for inexpensive prices. After all, you have the entire planet to choose from.

Outsourcing requires money, and it can add up quickly, especially if you publish more than one book.

Remember, you need to have your book proofread and edited; you need to create a cover — or more likely, more than one; you need to write an enticing book description for Amazon or wherever you're selling your book; you'll need to promote and market your manuscript; if you're doing book signings and speeches, then you may need to pay for travel expenses.

As you can see, the cost can add up quite quickly if you want to produce a good quality book and you want it to sell.

To help you in your efforts to become a professional writer who's making a living, you need to build a network and engage your audience.

The best way to build a network is to find other writers and form a relationship with them. Join writing groups on social media sites such as LinkedIn, Facebook, Google Plus, and so forth, and begin having conversations with writers and eventually you'll find a few who are willing to work with you in a partnership of sorts.

Don't forget about real-world places to meet writers such as bookstores, libraries, writing associations, your local Chamber of Commerce, networking groups, and meetup groups. These organizations (and many more) are useful to find kindred spirits who are willing to exchange services.

For example, within a network of writers, you can exchange books to proofread. You send them a copy of your book, perhaps chapter by chapter, to proofread, and they do the same and send their books to you.

If you can connect with some people who are skilled at graphics, you might offer to write or modify their website copy in exchange for art on a book cover.

Work your network for referrals as well. If you need to create a book cover, put the word out to your writing network and more than likely you'll soon find yourself hooked up with a good book cover artist.

Chapter 14
Networking

One of the keys to making this work is that you need to be willing to give as well as to receive. When another writer asks you for referral, you need to be willing to give it to them.

To keep your group engaged, I have found the best thing to do is to create a Facebook group. Post frequently, at least once a day, otherwise the group may become inactive. In other words, stir the pot occasionally or find a couple of motivated members who will do it for you.

You might be tempted use your team to help you get reviews on your books, but avoid that temptation. Amazon's terms and conditions about book reviews explicitly don't allow friends or business associates to review each other's books. Creating a group to trade book reviews is a clear violation of the terms and conditions and could get your Amazon account suspended or even deleted.

However, nothing prevents you from getting reviews or testimonials from your team for other purposes. For example, you might ask a team member to write a book review for your website or to include in your promotional copy.

Just be careful that you thoroughly understand the terms and conditions of any place you post reviews of this nature. Obviously, if you put them on your own blog or in your own promotional materials there won't be a problem.

For a one to one exchange, such as "I'll proofread chapter 4 of your book if you proofread chapter 12 of mine", an oral agreement is just fine. After all, there's not that much to lose.

However, I've learned through hard experience that for more complicated or long-lasting exchanges, a written agreement is generally best. This agreement, while it doesn't have to be a legal document, should spell out what's expected of both parties, timing, and so forth.

For example, if you create an exchange with another writer to write an article for their blog every other week in exchange for proofreading, write up a memo stating who does what, under what conditions, and for how long. Otherwise, the exchange tends to become muddy and hard feelings probably result.

Building a team of fellow writers and other creative people is a great way to leverage the power of many to help you succeed as a professional writer. It gives you more than twenty-four hours in a day because you are using hours from other people's days.

TAKE PART IN WRITING ASSOCIATIONS

One of the best ways to network is to take part in writing associations. There are associations at a local level, often working with libraries, for whole states, regions, and even nationally. Most, if not all, of them have Internet sites to allow you to network online.

A few of them that I've found useful are listed below.

Chapter 14
Networking

THE ALLIANCE OF INDEPENDENT AUTHORS
This organization operates throughout the world, and is dedicated to helping self-publishing writers and authors who provide services.

http://smooth.li/alli

NONFICTION AUTHORS ASSOCIATION
The Nonfiction Authors Association provides services to nonfiction authors by putting on teleseminars, posting articles and providing services.

http://smooth.li/naa
https://twitter.com/NonfictionAssoc

AUTHORS GUILD
The Authors Guide provides support for authors and maintains a community where you can find help if you need it.

https://authorsguild.org/

BUSINESS CARDS
Spend the time to create quality business cards. By this I mean hire a graphics artist or designer to work with you to create a business card which projects your image precisely.

Sure, you can jump online to one of those online self-service companies and order a box of plain Jane, same as everybody else boring cards. In fact, when you're first starting out and you have a small budget, that's exactly the thing to do.

However, as soon as you have enough money in your budget, after you've secured your blog hosting and a few other things, spend the money and do it right.

Your business card needs to present you in the best possible light. It needs to have the correct colors and fonts, your logo, and the proper combination of these things to promote your self-publishing and author brands.

You can expect to spend a couple of hundred dollars or more getting your cards designed, although in many cases it is possible to trade your writing services for their design services.

Create business cards that you'll be proud to hand out to everyone, that you feel so good about that they practically fly out of your hands.

Don't hesitate to pass out your business cards wherever you go. They don't do any good sitting in a box in a drawer in your house or in the trunk of your car. Hand them out to everyone, but make sure you give each person a firm handshake, find out their name, and strike up a conversation with them, even if it only last for a few minutes. In other words, give them a reason to keep your business card on the top of their pile rather than throwing it into a drawer where it rots for years' unseen and unused.

One of the great things about having business cards is that it adds to the feeling that your company and your business is real. Having a card with your well-designed logo, your selection of fonts and colors, and your contact information is part of being in business and doing it well.

Besides, in the world of networking, there is little worse than being asked for a business card and having to make some lame excuse as to why you don't have one.

Oh yes, I know that these days many smartphones let people exchange contact information by tapping their screens together. As a computer security expert, that kind of interaction between my phone and your phone makes me shudder.

Business cards work much better because they are physical, tangible assets. You can hand them to people, shake their hand, and introduce yourself. It's hard to do that with a cell phone.

CONCLUSIONS

If you want to make a good living as a self-published author, spend the time to build up a network of other authors and people who have the same interests as you.

By doing this, you'll expand the amount of work you can get done, and get access to resources and people that otherwise would be out of reach.

Writing associations are among the best ways to network, because if you leverage them properly you have access to hundreds or even thousands of like-minded people.

Reaching out to other people and helping them is the best way to build your network. Don't worry about getting things in return – that will happen soon enough.

Get involved in your local community, the writing community, and the communities associated with your genre, and you will find allies willing to help you expand your career.

Nobody succeeds alone. Everyone who became famous, rich, successful, or powerful did so with the help of others.

Networking is one of the most powerful tools available to a self-published author. Start doing it today.

Chapter 15
Keep the Money Flowing

To make a living as a self-published author, you must create a steady, consistent income. While getting an occasional book that sells very well or even becomes a bestseller is very fulfilling, it's much more important to produce books that sell moderately well week after week over a long period of time.

The next challenge that you'll face is building your writing and publishing "empire" up to the point where it is giving you a steady and respectable income. The difficulty is not necessarily creating a single book that sells well — with some hard work, a strong focus, some great promotion, and a little bit of luck you can make it sells very well for short time.

My first bestseller, *Focus on LinkedIn*, did exceptionally well. Because I had gotten many reviews and promoted heavily using a service (which no longer exists), I could sell a thousand copies within a single day. Building on that success, I quickly submitted the book to BookBub, was accepted, and sold another five thousand copies.

Unfortunately, the book tanked after that and I have never been able to rebuild that success with that title. Sure, the book sells well when priced at ninety-nine cents and is blasted to a targeted email list consisting of 440 thousand addresses. However, when priced at a more respectable point, $4.99, sales dropped until the book is selling just a few copies a week.

Chapter 15
Keep the Money Flowing

That experience is not unique among self-published authors. A friend of mine published a coloring book which she promoted heavily at a highly-reduced price. She sold over two thousand copies in a few days. However, when the book was priced to the point where she can make a decent royalty, sales dropped and never recovered.

Make no mistake about it, selling a few hundred or a few thousand copies of your title in a very short time feels very good, and even priced at ninety-nine cents you make a good chunk of change.

But you can't run a business that way — spikes and valleys in your income make it hard to predict how much you're going to make from day to day, week to week and month to month. Unpredictable income makes it hard to pay predictable bills such as rent, credit cards, car payments and utilities.

Thus, your focus should be on creating a writing and publishing business which produces a stream of income which is predictable and relatively secure.

Two important points to consider are:

- One or two books can go up and down in sales rapidly and sometimes unpredictably.
- The more books you publish, the more this tendency will even-out.

As I've stressed several times in this book, your focus should be on producing many quality books as fast as possible.

Additionally, there are opportunities for income from sources other than just the royalties from selling your book.

We'll go over some of the options that are available for helping you produce a steady, relatively predictable stream of income from your self-publishing career.

WRITE AS MANY BOOKS AS FAST AS YOU CAN

Regardless of whether you write fiction or nonfiction, illustrate children's books, publish coloring or puzzle books, or produce comic books, to create a reliable income — the prerequisite for quitting your full-time job — you need to focus on quantity.

Quantity is more important than quality and quality is more important than length.

What does that mean?

LENGTH

Let's begin with length. What is the ideal length for a book? If you're trying to make a living as a self-published author, it turns out that shorter is better — up to a point. Look at it this way, you can probably write, publish, promote and sell ten 10,000 word books in less time than it takes to write one 100,000-word book.

For example, suppose you spend six months writing 100,000-word novel, then you publish it and promote it to the world. For that entire six months, your novel is not producing any income. When you publish the book, you'll probably price it at something like $9.95 for the Kindle version and $16.95 for the

Chapter 15
Keep the Money Flowing

paperback, and you may sell a few hundred or even a thousand copies.

On the other hand, if you wrote eight 10,000 word books that each took three weeks to write, proofread, publish and promote, then you would begin making money, at least potentially, within three weeks of beginning that process.

You'd probably price one of these smaller books at $3.99 for the Kindle version and $6.95 for the paperback. At the much lower price point, with some moderate promotion, you probably sell anywhere from a few dozen to a few hundred copies a month.

Thus, if you sold 10 Kindle copies and 5 paperbacks of the 100,000-word novel, your gross sales would $184.25 and your royalties probably around $100.

On shorter books, if you sold the same number of each, gross profits would be $74.65 each, or $597.20 total for all of them.

In this simplified example, not only would you make over three times the income from the smaller books, but you'd begin earning money on the publication of the first one on the third week rather than after six months of writing.

This also means you have more chances of "getting it right." With only one novel after six months, you are taking a big gamble regarding time that the book will sell well enough to justify that much work. If the book doesn't sell well, then you will have lost all that time with little to show for it.

On the other hand, with eight books you have more chances to succeed. One of those eight might sell very well, 2 or 3 might sell okay, and the other 4 could bomb. But at least you have the potential to get income after the third week (in this example).

Kindle readers (at least) prefer shorter books; they tend to favor quick reads that they can digest over lunch or in an evening than a long novel or non-fiction volume.

The point is to focus on creating books in the 10,000 to 15,000-word range in general.

QUALITY

Even though quantity is more important than quality in the world of self-publishing, that doesn't mean that you shouldn't spend the time and effort to ensure that your book is a high quality and presents good value to your readers.

A poor-quality book that is rife with misspellings and grammar errors, that is poorly organized, and doesn't provide value to your readers can sabotage your self-publishing career.

Take pride in your work, and make it show by producing the best books that you can possibly produce.

Make sure you proofread your books for grammar and spelling errors. Modern word processors, at least if they are any good, include reasonable grammar and spelling checkers. Take advantage of them to catch a few errors.

Use a service such as grammarly.com and autocrit.com, among others, to further check your work for errors.

Chapter 15
Keep the Money Flowing

Before sending your book to anyone else to read, it's a good idea to read through the entire thing out loud twice, on separate days. I'm constantly amazed at how many errors I uncover by the simple fact of having read it out loud.

Hiring another person to proofread your book is a good idea, and you'll have to decide whether the benefit is worth the cost. There are many good proofreaders on Fiverr.com that will proofread your book for very good rates.

If you can't afford a proofreader, or if you don't expect to sell enough books to justify the cost, then see if you can exchange services (barter) with another writing friend and get them to proofread it for you.

Make sure your book is formatted properly and contains the appropriate front and back material organized correctly.

Take the time to put together a quality table of contents – most word processors will do this for you.

Don't forget about your book cover, your Amazon Book page, your Author Central pages, your book trailer, and everything else that goes with it. For every single book that you produce, these things need to be of high quality and complete.

A poor book cover will stop your sales cold in their tracks and make you look unprofessional and amateurish. More than a handful of grammar or spelling errors will make you look sloppy and undermine your credibility. A poorly-written book description can reduce your sales dramatically, and amateurish leak? produced book trailer will be ignored and not help with sales as you intended.

Keep in mind, however, that these things cost money and time. For every book, you should strike a balancing act between quality and speed of production.

Authors tend to write books because they feel passionate about subjects, and because they want to make money. Both motivations demand that you deliver a high-quality product. Create the best product that you can, within the timeframe and with the resources that you have available.

QUANTITY
We've discussed this several times already, so I won't spend a lot of time belaboring the point. As a self-published author, the best way to make a living is to publish high-quality books as often as you can. As a rule, the more books you publish, the more money you're going to make.

Thus, put in a writing routine that lets you write and publish books quickly while still promoting and doing all the other tasks that you need to do for all your other books.

BECOME AN AMAZON AFFILIATE
If you have not done this already, stop reading this book and go become an Amazon affiliate. You can make a bit of extra money by becoming an affiliate and adding your tag to each of your book links.

Use the link below to proceed to the Amazon affiliate site.

http://smooth.li/amazon

Chapter 15
Keep the Money Flowing

Create your affiliate account, which is attached to your regular Amazon account, and get your affiliate ID.

Use this affiliate ID in your Amazon book links (and if you sell anything else from Amazon, use it there as well).

A sample affiliate link is shown below:

> https://www.amazon.com/dp/1943517428/?tag=thewritingkin-20

The number "1943517428" is the ASIN or ISBN number of the book or product. The text after the "/?tag=" is your affiliate ID as it is assigned by Amazon. The "-20", which is part of your affiliate ID, is the country code.

You can find out more about the link format for the Amazon affiliate program on the page below:

> http://smooth.li/amazonlinks

TAKE ADVANTAGE OF AMAZON AFFILIATE SALES

Once you have your affiliate ID, use it in all your advertising and promotional links. By doing this, you'll receive a small commission for everything (not just your books) that someone buys during that session on Amazon.

For example, if you post some promotion on Facebook about your book with a link to its page on Amazon, be sure to use your affiliate ID in that link. This way if someone clicks on the link, you make a little bit of extra money on your book. In fact, even if they don't buy your book, you'll make extra money on everything else that they purchase.

Use the Amazon affiliate links for your own social media posts, your blog, and anything else that you have control over.

However, when you give your link out to other people, or post it on other websites, don't include the affiliate tag. This is because Amazon searches the web for links to book pages (and other product page as well) and uses that to determine the ranking within categories. In that case, you want a bare-bones link to your book, which would look something like this:

https://www.amazon.com/dp/1943517428/

By using Amazon Affiliate links for your books, you can add anywhere from a few dollars to a few hundred dollars each month to your income. It's a nice way to make a few extra bucks for very little work, and sometimes, you'll get lucky and someone will make a big purchase and you'll make a lot of money.

SELL STUFF

An important factor in determining how much profit you make off your books is through sales of additional products and services. There's nothing wrong with recommending anything that you feel as value for your readers regardless of whether you make profit from them.

You do have to be careful to ensure that you have no conflicts of interest, meaning that you shouldn't recommend anything just because you're making money from it. Rather, the profit you make should be incidental to your recommendation.

Chapter 15
Keep the Money Flowing

Think about your book, and I'm sure you'll come up with products and services that your readers can use that are related to your genre or subject.

For example:

- The author of a Christian book could recommend a Bible that they found to be particularly enlightening.
- In a book about writing, a course on grammar could be recommended.
- A survival book might recommend tools to help the reader survive in the event of a disaster.

You get the idea, don't you?

Any courses that you used to become skilled or knowledgeable about the subject of your book are certainly fair game for you to recommend to your readers.

Products that you feel are helpful to your readers, if they are pertinent to the subject at hand, can be recommended.

To do this, become an affiliate of those products and services that you want to recommend, and then include the links provided by the vendor within your book. Make sure that you note that the link is an affiliate link and that you will make a commission if a purchase is made. This is required by the FTC.

A common tactic to increase your profits is to create additional products that fit in with the theme of your book. For example, a book about LinkedIn could end with an offer for a more in-depth course on how to create a LinkedIn profile and use it effectively. If you wrote a book on surviving disasters, you could also create a course to going to more detail what you offered for sale at the end of the book.

Don't overdo it, because you don't want to give your readers the impression that your book is just a catalog or a way to get them to buy additional products and services. Think about it: would you pay money for a catalog or sales brochure? Don't do that to your readers.

WATCH YOUR STATISTICS

It's important to keep an eye on your statistics. You have at your disposal the KDP dashboard, the CreateSpace dashboard, the ACX dashboard, and the Amazon affiliates dashboard. By putting all these together, you can get a good idea of how your books are doing.

Each of these dashboards is totally different from the other, and none of them really presents the information in the most useful format. KDP is the most difficult to interpret, because you have the option of seeing all the statistics in summary, or each one individually.

CreateSpace, on the other hand, lets you see the breakdown for each month for each book, which is exactly the information you want.

KDpulse is a nice little product that installs into your browser as a plug-in that list each book individually by different time periods. This product only examines your KDP sale statistics, which is your Kindle format e-books.

> http://smooth.li/kdpulse

I recommend making it a point to examine your sales statistics at the end of each day. Pick a consistent time, and take a screenshot of your CreateSpace and ACX sales statistics. This way you'll be able to compare sales from day to day.

It's important to track your sales on a consistent basis, either daily or weekly, because if the sales of a book dip, you'll want to be able to know that right away, so you can investigate the reasons why. It could be as simple as a promotion ended, or as complicated as someone else published a book on the same topic and category which took away some of your own sales.

You'll also begin to learn the pattern of your sales. For example, *Focus on LinkedIn* has better sales on the weekend than on weekdays, whereas *How to Sell on eBay* is exactly the opposite.

Higher sales could be for any number of reasons:

- A promotion.
- The book moved up in ranking.
- Amazon noticed it's been selling well and is promoting it.
- An external event has caused a surge in sales.
- You added it to AMS (Amazon Marketing Services).

Reasons why sales can fall include:

- No promotion.
- A failed promotion.
- The book moved down in ranking.
- You removed the book from AMS or changed its keywords.
- Amazon removed it from a category.
- Amazon suspended the book (this will result in no sales).
- Amazon stopped promoting it.
- A competing book is taking some of the sales.
- It is a holiday (sales typically drop on a holiday).
- Some external event has occurred (such as a national disaster, a baseball game or an election).

Sometimes you can figure out why the sales of a book have changed, and sometimes it can be very obscure. What is important is when sales drop, you should investigate and act accordingly, keeping in mind that sometimes sales drop temporarily for some reasons (such as a national emergency).

CONTINUOUS LEARNING

To stay ahead of the game, you must be willing to educate yourself and learn constantly. There are many courses available all over the web, some of them good, and some of them not so good.

I found it best to take small courses, sometimes as short as an hour, on specific topics. These courses generally are inexpensive, and since they're so short, I can always find time to get through them.

Udemy.com has many thousands of courses on every conceivable subject. I found the quality is good, the courses are short and straightforward, and they stick to the point.

> http://smooth.li/udemy
> *Note, this is an affiliate link. If you purchase the product I will receive a small commission*

Udemy as frequent sales, lowering the price of courses to $10 or $15 in some cases. Get on their mailing list, and wait for the sales or coupons.

Continuing education is vital for you to prosper as a self-published author. I've taken literally over 100 courses in the past couple of years to learn the ins and outs of writing, self-publishing, editing, creating book covers, graphics, and dozens of other subjects related one way or another to self-publishing and writing books.

However, be on your guard because some courses offer "get rich quick" or "make zillions of dollars in less than a minute" and so forth. I've taken my fair share of these, and what I've learned from experience that what is successful at making a living as a self-published author is walking the walk — in other words, doing the work.

Chapter 15
Keep the Money Flowing

AVOID THE SCAMS AND SCHEMES

With virtually any field that exists, there are many individuals and businesses who offer services and products of one form or another. Quite often, what they offer has value and, if you make use of them, will give you a good return on investment.

Others offer snake oil and witches' brews that sound excellent but wind up being complete waste of money and, more importantly, time.

When I first started my writing career, I really didn't know which direction was best. Somehow, I got on all the email lists of people who sell money-making type products, especially those that specialize in writing and publishing.

The offers that get sent out on the list are very attractive and their marketing promotional materials are written in such a way as to make them almost irresistible. Think of the most enticing infomercials or the shopping channels and you'll get the idea.

The way most of these work is they send out an invitation to a one hour webinar which gives away a few secrets or some information. Sometimes these webinars are very useful and what they teach can be used, but they always contain hooks into one or more products that are extremely attractively packaged.

As it turned out, one of the very first webinars that I attended was for an extraordinarily useful service that I continue to use. This was the Author Audience Academy by Shelley Hitz. She sold a yearly subscription to her classes on how to write,

Chapter 15
Keep the Money Flowing

publish and promote nonfiction books. Her classes are incredibly valuable, and are one of the few that I recommend.

I say this to illustrate that occasionally these webinars lead to useful products and services at a reasonable cost. Additionally, the webinars themselves are often worth watching just for the information in them.

I went through a period where I bought most of the products and services that seemed like they would be even marginally useful, if the price was relatively low.

Some of these products work out very well, and by adding them to my toolkit I've improved my business. Some of those are recommended within this book.

The point of this is that my intention is to help you establish and grow your self-published writing career with the knowledge that I've gained combined with recommendations of specific tools, books and products that I found to be of service.

In other words, I've already negotiated the minefield and laid down some tape on the ground for you to follow so you don't have to experience the explosions in the same way that I did.

Attending the webinars and reading the promotional materials for these products and services can give you some value.

I use the following rules, learned through hard experience, before purchasing any of these products:

- They must offer a no questions asked, money back guarantee. My feeling is if the product doesn't work or doesn't operate as advertised, or you simply don't like it, the money should be returned.
- The product or service must be usable standing on its own without any upsells. An upsell is an additional, extra cost option which is often very useful. Just make sure that the original product gives the value promised without purchasing the upsell.
- Obviously, the cost must be reasonable, given the value returned.
- This is the most important criteria: is the product going to sit on your hard drive and collect dust or are you going to use it? Collecting applications, PDF files, books, classes, webinars and so forth without using them is a losing game when you're trying to create a career.
-

ETHICS

A discussion about pursuing a career in writing, or any career for that matter, wouldn't be complete without a section about ethics.

Consider this definition of ethics from Merriam-Webster:

the principles of conduct governing an individual or a group <professional ethics>

Morals and ethics have different connotations, as described in the usage note below.

Chapter 15
Keep the Money Flowing

> ... morals usually connote an element of subjective preference, while ethics tends to suggest aspects of universal fairness and the question of whether an action is responsible:

You'll run into various ethical questions as your career progresses. Some of these will be obvious and simple, and others will be subtler, perhaps falling into an ethically gray area.

If someone asks you to sabotage the computers of a client that was not paying their bills, you would almost certainly refuse. This is clear-cut.

Ethical questions often aren't that obvious, and sometimes even work in reverse.

For example, everyone needs a good work/life balance, regardless of whether they are hourly employees or paid a flat salary. Often, employers hire salaried employees expressly for working them more than normal work hours. After all, the more hours the corporation to get out of a salaried employee, the lower the cost of that employee.

This is an ethical dilemma that I've had to face many times throughout my thirty-five-year career. Do I put in the extra hours, generally required because of inadequate resource and time estimates, or do I appear to be "not a team member" and refuse?

Consider that by going along with the flow and working extra hours you are in effect allowing your manager to succeed with their poor estimates. Is that the most ethical thing to do?

Because every time you put in a heroic effort to complete inadequately staffed projects or deadlines that don't make sense, you are reinforcing your manager's habit of depending upon overtime to meet schedules.

Of course, you should weigh this against possible disciplinary action from your employer.

In the world of writing, there are many similar ethical issues.

Do you ensure that you have properly researched your material? And if so, did you properly cite everything, even if it was paraphrased?

Do you define deadlines and schedules for all phases of your book from the idea, all the way through to promotion after publication?

Do you allow yourself to give into writer's block? The inability to write can be caused by many different factors, including invalidations and evaluations, and improper or incomplete understanding of your material, too many distractions, improper diet, not enough sleep, and editing while writing. I'm sure there are many other reasons as well.

However, because you stated that you want to be a professional self-publishing author, you can't give into writer's block. Doing so creates an ethical situation, especially if your income depends upon your writing or other skills.

Have you proofread your book? While it's true that a book does not have to be perfect, it's a good idea to go through your manuscript at least twice to ensure that it meets your standards of quality. Then get a second pair of eyes to read it over. Writers are too close to their own works to be good proofreaders.

Is your book truthful? There are many ways to bend the truth. On one of my ghostwriting projects, the client was very angry and wanted to stress the faults and hurts from others. Since there are always multiple sides to every story, this created a series of untruths in the book. It's important to be sure that your work is well-balanced and includes multiple points of view, if only to demonstrate that they are incorrect.

Have you betrayed any confidences? In general, it's a good idea to forgo including anything told to you in confidence in your books. There are exceptions, but think about them carefully before proceeding. For example, if you're writing a book about child abuse, then you probably will be discussing things that were told to you in confidence, if only by the abuser. Just ensure that would you write about is necessary for you to tell your story, and that you don't harm those who are innocent.

Are all your related materials well done? Is the quality of your book cover top-of-the-line? Have you done a good job on your Amazon (or other publisher) book description? Are your title and subtitle as good as they can be? These things are important to book sales, and if any of them are substandard, then your sales will be affected.

Are you regularly maintaining your blog? A blog is essential for a self-published author. It's important to ensure that you have one of the articles written on a regular basis.

Are you actively working your audience? To sell your books, you must spend time communicating with your audience. You can do this with the Facebook group or page, from your blog, via email, and any number of other means. It's true that the more that people are interested in you and your message, the more they will purchase your books.

Is your bookkeeping up-to-date? Are you paying your taxes regularly and on time? Do you know from month to month, or better yet from week to week, how well you're doing financially? It is important to understand how well your books are selling at any point in time. If sales slump, you need to do something to fix it. On the other hand, if your sales go up, you want to know what you did to make that happen so you can do it again.

These are just a few of the ethical issues that come to mind, and I'm sure that you can think of many others.

The point is that the cleaner you can keep your ethics, the better you're going to do. It might seem expedient to skip doing a little research or work extra hours late into the evening to meet a deadline, but is that really the right thing to do? Skipping research might come back to haunt you later in the form of bad Amazon reviews or even lawsuits. Working too late for long periods of time can result in writer's block, stress, and even health issues.

Finally, I want to mention that there is often a temptation to create works that are themselves ethically questionable.

This includes pyramid schemes, scams, slanderous works, books written using automated software, get rich schemes,

Chapter 15
Keep the Money Flowing

and so forth. While it can seem like you'll make a lot of money writing a book about and promoting that wonderful moneymaking scheme that you have dreamed up, just make sure that it's legal and that it really does work as described.

If you want to make a long-term career as a self-published author, or anything else for that matter, it is absolutely vital that you remain ethical at all times.

If something feels wrong, it probably is wrong.

If you want to do something and it makes you feel uneasy, take another look at it – and you'll probably find it violates your code of ethics in some way.

If it appears too good to be true, look for the lie.

Being ethical is the best way to remain happy and keep your career on track.

CONCLUSIONS

Writing books is a great place to start to make a career as a self-published author. The best strategy is to write as many high-quality books on topics that are of interest to others as you can.

Quality is critical. Speed of publication is vital. You can use those two factors to build a relatively nice income as a writer.

However, in this chapter we've only scratched on the surface of other ways that you can use your writing to bring in income.

The idea was to give you some ideas about how you can leverage your books to create even more profits.

Some of the ways that we haven't gone into detail on include:

- Build a retreat around a book and invite people to attend for a fee. Many Christian or motivational authors use this tactic to use their book to get their message out to the public.
- There is nothing more powerful than a book to enhance your credibility in any field. The public looks up to people who have written books, and considers them to be leaders and knowledgeable on the subject. You can use this to help with your career or business.
- Create additional products related to the topic of your books. You can create checklists, templates, courses, lectures, and just about anything else that makes sense in context.
- Monetize your blog by including advertising or selling products.
- Sell products and services in your email newsletter.

I think you get the idea. Your book should be a base on which you build an even greater income and a business. By treating it that way, rather than just depending upon royalties, you can create yourself a very nice and stable living.

Chapter 16
It's a Business

Treat your writing career as a business. If you're depending upon your income as a self-published author, then you need to take it seriously and ensure you are running it as a real business, and not as a hobby.

BUSINESS LICENSE

In most localities, you need to purchase a local business license, and if you're working out of your home, you may need to purchase a permit to allow you to do that. Your local City Hall, or the equivalent, will have details on the process and fees.

LOCAL TAXES

Some localities require you to pay local business taxes. Make sure you visit your city or county website to ensure that you understand your legal requirements and filing steps.

STATE AND FEDERAL TAXES

Any income you make is taxable over the state and federal level. Keep good records of all your income and expenses.

A service such as QuickBooks – the self-employed version is very affordable – can be very helpful in organizing the record-keeping associated with your small business. You can use this to record all the financial details of your business. Better still, QuickBooks can read in the information from your credit cards and bank accounts and give you the opportunity to categorize that based upon personal or business expenses.

Chapter 16
It's a Business

Keep in mind that being a self-published author means you are self-employed — even if you or full-time employed at another job. This means you can write off expenses such as part of your home is a home office, health insurance premiums, communications, and part of your car, among other things. It's best to go over this with an accountant who will fill you in on what you can and can't write off.

If you publish through Amazon – KD, CreateSpace or ACX – you'll receive the appropriate tax forms from them at the end of the year. They will also report all your income to the IRS (or the equivalent for other countries) and other government agencies as required.

HOME OFFICE

If you are a self-published author and you work from home, you can write off a percentage of the cost of your living space on your taxes.

Make sure you define a certain area of your home or apartment as your home office and keep it segregated. A separate room or even a part of a room is ideal.

BUSINESS EXPENSES

Everything that you use for your business, from a single postage stamp all the way up to the computer that you use for word processing, is deductible on your income tax. Some of these items, such as a large computer, might require special handling on your taxes, so be sure to check with your tax accountant.

Working Hours

You might think that it's best to work anytime you want, willy-nilly, if you're self-employed. That can work for some people, but for most of us, it's best to define work hours to help keep the working life, even though it's self-employed, separate from the personal life. This way both you and your family – and your friends – will understand that during your "work hours" you are working and not to be bothered.

Backups

Make sure copies of your manuscripts, research notes, interviews, files, video files, and so forth are kept backed-up in multiple locations.

I recommend using a product such as Carbonite to keep a backup of all the data files on your computer. This application is installed on your Windows or Mac system and makes a copy of your work on a computer located somewhere else in the country. That way, if your computer is damaged or destroyed your work is safe.

> http://smooth.li/carbonite
> *Note, this is an affiliate link. If you purchase the product I will receive a small commission.*

Save Often

You might think this goes without saying, but it's important that as you're working on your manuscript you hit the save button regularly. I like to save after completing a page, or even more often than that.

You can also set Microsoft Word to automatically save your document regularly.

Chapter 16
It's a Business

This way if your computer or word processing program crashes you'll have a reasonably up-to-date copy of your manuscript. I tend to save every ten minutes or so, or after about 3 to 5 paragraphs of work.

DON'T SKIMP ON WHAT IS IMPORTANT

Money is always an issue for every business, and it's important to know where money should be spent and where it can be saved. Don't be a person who is penny wise and pound foolish. What this means is don't be one of those people who say that penny here and there while costing themselves real money in lost profits or opportunities.

Where should you spend your money?

- Spend the money to purchase good web hosting. I recommend Siteground because their hosting is rock solid stable, performs well in their support is excellent. For just a few dollars a month, probably less than a single cup of Starbucks coffee, you'll get a professional hosting service. This also comes with a free domain name (the first year) which you'll need to establish your brand.
- Hire a local professional to take the photos for your author biography and media kits.
- Hire a local professional designer to work with you to create a logo to establish your brand.
- Invest in a good computer for your word processing needs. As a professional writer, you'll be spending a good portion of every day typing on your computer, so

you want to make sure you have one that is reliable and fast.

- Investment a good chair to check your back. Again, much of your day will be spent sitting in front of your computer, which can be hell on your back.
- Spend the money to join organizations, as described in Writing Associations, to network with other writers in your area. This can be of immense help in furthering your writing career as you can find beta readers, people who will critique your work, proofreaders, and other specialties that you'll need.
- Invest in training either online or at your local community college to further your mind and skills.
- Work with good outsources to proofread your work, design, and create book covers and so forth.

CONTROL EXPENSES

On the other hand, keep unnecessary expenses under control. While it is important to is required for your business, is equally important to understand what isn't needed as well.

Resist the "shiny object syndrome." As you proceed through your writing career, and spend time researching on the Internet, you'll find many "money making" offers of all types. You'll see advertisements for training applications on how to create and sell puzzle books, coloring books, comic books, calendars, and just about anything else you can think of.

While some of these are completely valid and may help you make some money, the best strategy is to find your niche (or niches) and focus on that area instead of going for the quick buck and something that sounds really good in an advertisement or webinar.

Personally, I've spent more than I like to think about on shiny objects that I thought might help my writing career or short-circuit some of the work needed to make money in this field.

I can tell you from experience, just focus your attention on your goals and your niche, and be willing to change direction if that's not working out or if needed.

INCORPORATING

Check with your accounting or attorney to see if it's a good idea for you to incorporate your self-publishing business.

CONCLUSIONS

Are you planning to make a career out of being a self-published author?

If you answered yes, then ensure you treat it as a business. As soon as you decide it is or is going to be your career, you've also decided to create a business.

Treat it like one.

Conclusions

You can make a living, in fact you can make a good living, as a self-published author. Treat it the same as you would any other career – it's going to take education, training, practice, hard work, and networking with other like-minded professionals.

Where do you begin? Write your first book quickly while maintaining high quality. Set aside at least four hours every day, more if possible, or you can sequester yourself away from others and write your book. Yes, of course, you should do research before you begin to see if there's a market for the book, but don't over think it.

You see, that first book, getting it written and published, is a huge milestone for self-published author. It means you are successful! You've accomplished something that very few have done – you written and published a book.

Don't get discouraged if your first book doesn't sell; oh, you'll sell a few copies to friends, family members, coworkers, and others that you know, but very few first books sell more than a few dozen or a few hundred copies.

While you're writing that first book, start working on your author brand and platform. Create a blog and email list, and choose which social media is best for you.

Well before you publish, begin writing short, 300-word or so articles for your blog and social media about your book. You could take a paragraph from one chapter, put it in quotes, and

Conclusions

write a couple of paragraphs about what it means. Mention that this is from your up-and-coming book.

If you're feeling daring, make a video of yourself talking about your book. You can even have a friend interview you, if you want. Explain why you wrote it, what benefits it has for your readers, why you decided to become an author, and so forth. Remember to include the name of your blog and your book in the interview.

Post that video to YouTube and share it around your social media.

This will get you used to working with social media and building a buzz, as it's called, about the book you'll be publishing soon. More than likely, others in your friend list and groups will comment on these posts, which will enable you to give even more information.

Once your book is published, spend some time letting your friends, families, coworkers and other people know that you've written it and that it is now for sale on Amazon.

Then get started on your next book and use the lessons that you've learned from the first book to make the second book even better.

Continue this process until you have built a respectable blog with several dozen or more articles, you have more than 50 people on your email list, and you've been posting regularly to the social media of your choice.

Don't even think about purchasing any advertising, buying banner ads, or spending any money on promotion at all until your blog, author platform, email list, Amazon Author Central, and the other things talked about in this book are mature.

By that I mean that you have gained a following of people who are interested in what you have to say and want to read what you publish.

You might be ready to do this after your first book, your second, or may even take half a dozen. In my own case, I purchased paid advertising right away and wasted a lot of money. In hindsight, my author platform and related materials were not mature until I had completed a dozen books.

The most important thing is to keep at it. Continue to write books, publish them, and work your blog, email list, and social media. Keep communicating with your readers, and continue to build your network of authors and other like-minded professionals.

In volume 2 of this series, will be talking about promotion. Everything we've discussed in the first volume is laying the foundation for promoting yourself and your books.

Any money that you spend on advertising or promotion before the foundation is laid and solid is almost certainly wasted.

Volume 3 will give you all the steps that you need to follow when you find that you have a book that isn't selling. There are reasons why books don't sell – the cover could be unappealing, the title could be wrong, the "look inside" might

Conclusions

be inappropriate, the description could be wrong, or the subtitle could be off.

In the worst case, it could just be that a book has been written about a topic of which there is no interest. I would imagine that a book about how to peel potatoes wouldn't sell very well. Volume 3 will go into all the reasons why books don't sell and give you the steps needed to take corrective action.

Good luck on your journey, and get started writing your first book if you haven't already. Get it published, build your author platform, engage your audience, and keep going. Don't let anybody get in your way – you can make it if you put in the effort, get the education, and do the right things.

Before you go

If you scroll to the last page in this eBook, you will have the opportunity to leave feedback and share the book with Before You Go. I'd be grateful if you turned to the last page and shared the book.

Also, if you have time, please leave a review. Positive reviews are incredibly useful. If you didn't like the book, please email me at rich@thewritingking.com and I'd be happy to get your input.

References

Berg, David. n.d. "Libel vs. Slander: Different Types of Defamation." *Nolo.* Accessed December 19, 2016. http://www.nolo.com/legal-encyclopedia/libel-vs-slander-different-types-defamation.html.

Clayton, Melinda. 2016. "Moving Print Book Files from CreateSpace to IngramSpark." *Indies Unlimited.* December 14. http://www.indiesunlimited.com/2016/12/14/moving-print-book-files-from-createspace-to-ingramspark/.

Crabben, Jan van der. 2011. "Alphabet." *Ancient History Encyclopedia.* April 28. Accessed 02 19, 2017. http://www.ancient.eu/alphabet/.

Drucker, Peter. 2006. *The Practice of Management (First published 1954).* Harper Business. Accessed December 31, 2016.

Ferreras, Jesse. 2015. "'Fifty Shades Of Grey' Was Written On A Blackberry." *Huff Post Business Canada.* February 19. Accessed JJanuary 1, 2017. http://www.huffingtonpost.ca/2015/02/19/fifty-shades-of-grey-blackberry_n_6709198.html.

Friedman, Jane. 2010. "Audience Development: Critical to Every Writer's Future." *Writer UnBoxed.* Februrary 19. Accessed January 6, 2017. http://writerunboxed.com/2010/02/19/audience-development-critical-to-every-writers-future/.

References

n.d. "Legal Terms and Definitions." *The People's Law Dictionary.*
    Accessed December 19, 2016.
    http://dictionary.law.com/default.aspx?selected=458.

Medina, John. 2015. "Vision." *Brain Rules.* Accessed January 7,
    2017. http://www.brainrules.net/vision.

Templeton, Brad. 2008. "10 Big Myths about copyright explained."
    Brad Templeton. October. Accessed December 19, 2016.

n.d. "The Gutenberg Press." *Treasures of the McDonald Collection.*
    http://scarc.library.oregonstate.edu/omeka/exhibits/show/m
    cdonald/incunabula/gutenberg/.

About the Author

https://www.linkedin.com/in/richardlowejr
Feel free to send a connection request

Follow me on Twitter: @richardlowejr

Richard Lowe has leveraged more than 35 years of experience as a Senior Computer Manager and Designer at four companies into that of a bestselling author, blogger, ghostwriter, and public speaker. He has written hundreds of articles for blogs and ghostwritten more than a dozen books and has published manuscripts about computers, the Internet, surviving disasters, management, and human rights. He is currently working on a ten-volume science fiction series – the Peacekeeper Series – to be published at the rate of three volumes per year, beginning in 2016.

Richard started in the field of Information Technology, first as the Vice President of Consulting at Software Techniques, Inc. Because he craved action, after six years he moved on to work for two companies at the same time: he was the Vice President of Consulting at Beck Computer Systems and the Senior Designer at BIF Accutel. In January 1994, Richard found a home at Trader Joe's as the Director of Technical Services and Computer Operations. He remained with that incredible company for almost 20 years before taking an early retirement to begin a new life as a professional writer. He is currently the CEO of The Writing King, a company that provides all forms of writing services, the owner of The EBay King, and a Senior Branding Expert for LinkedIn Makeover. You can find a current list of all books on his Author Page and

About the Author

take a look at his exclusive line of coloring books at The Coloring King.

Richard has a quirky sense of humor and has found that life is full of joy and wonder. As he puts it, "This little ball of rock, mud, and water we call Earth is an incredible place, with many secrets to discover. Beings fill our corner of the universe, and some are happy, and others are sad, but each has their unique story to tell."

His philosophy is to take life with a light heart, and he approaches each day as a new source of happiness. Evil is ignored, discarded, or defeated; good is helped, enriched, and fulfilled. One of his primary interests is to educate people about their human rights and assist them to learn how to be happy in life.

Richard spent many happy days hiking in national parks, crawling over boulders, and peering at Indian pictographs. He toured the Channel Islands off Santa Barbara and stared in fascination at wasps building their homes in Anza-Borrego. One of his joys is photography, and he has photographed more than 1,200 belly dancing events, as well as dozens of Renaissance fairs all over the country.

Because writing is his passion, Richard remains incredibly creative and prolific; each day he writes between 5,000 and 10,000 words, diligently using language to bring life to the world so that others may learn and be entertained.

Richard is the CEO of The Writing King, which specializes in fulfilling any writing need. You can find out more at https://www.thewritingking.com/, and emails are welcome at rich@thewritingking.com

Books by Richard G Lowe Jr.

Business Professional Series

On the Professional Code of Ethics and Business Conduct in the Workplace – Professional Ethics: 100 Tips to Improve Your Professional Life - have you ever wondered what it takes to be successful in the professional world? This book gives you some tips that will improve your job and your career.

Help! My Boss is Whacko! - How to Deal with a Hostile Work Environment - sometimes the problem is the boss. There are all kinds of managers, some competent, some incompetent, and others just plain whacked. This book will help you understand and handle those different types of managers.

Help! I've Lost My Job: Tips on What to do When You're Unexpectedly Unemployed – suddenly having to leave your job can be a harsh and emotional time in your life. Learn some of the things that you need to consider and handle if this happens to you.

Help! My Job Sucks Insider Tips on Making Your Job More Satisfying and Improving Your Career – sometimes conditions conspire to make the regular trek to a job feel like a trip through Dante's Inferno. Sometimes, these are out of our control, such as a malicious manager or incompetent colleague. On the other hand, we can take control of our lives and workplace and improve our situation. Get this book to learn what you can do when your job sucks.

Books by Richard G Lowe Jr.

How to Manage a Consulting Project: Make money, get your project done on time, and get referred again and again – I found that being a consultant is a great way to earn a living. Managing a consulting project can be a challenge. This book contains some tips to help you so you can deliver a better product or service to your customers.

How to be a Good Manager and Supervisor, and How to Delegate – Lessons Learned from the Trenches: Insider Secrets for Managers and Supervisors – I've been a manager for over thirty years I learned many things about how to get the job done and deliver quality service. The information in this book will help you manage your projects to a high level of quality.

Focus on LinkedIn – Learn how to create a LinkedIn profile and to network effectively using the #1 business social media site.

Home Computer Security Series

Safe Computing is Like Safe Sex: You have to practice it to avoid infection – Security expert and Computer Executive, Richard Lowe, presents the simple steps you can take to protect your computer, photos and information from evil doers and viruses. Using easy-to-understand examples and simple explanations, Lowe explains why hackers want your system, what they do with your information, and what you can do to keep them at bay. Lowe answers the question: how to you keep yourself say in the wild west of the internet.

Disaster Preparation and Survival Series

Real World Survival Tips and Survival Guide: Preparing for and Surviving Disasters with Survival Skills – CERT (Civilian Emergency Response Team) trained and Disaster Recovery Specialist, Richard Lowe, lays out how to make you, your family, and your friends ready for any disaster, large or small. Based upon specialized training, interviews with experts and personal experience, Lowe answers the big question: what is the secret to improving the odds of survival even after a big disaster?

Creating a Bug Out Bag to Save Your Life: What you need to pack for emergency evacuations - When you are ordered to evacuate—or leave of your free will—you probably won't have a lot of time to gather your belongings and the things you'll need. You may have just a few minutes to get out of your home. The best preparation for evacuation is to create what is called a bug out bag. These are also known as go-bags, as in, "grab it and go!"

Professional Freelance Writer Series

How to Operate a Freelance Writing Business, and How to be a Ghostwriter – Proven Tips and Tricks Every Author Needs to Know about Freelance Writing: Insider Secrets from a Professional Ghostwriter – This book explains how to be a ghostwriter, and gives tips on everything from finding customers to creating a statement of work to delivering your final product.

How to Write a Blog That Sells and How to Make Money From Blogging: Insider Secrets from a Professional Blogger:

Books by Richard G Lowe Jr.

Proven Tips and Tricks Every Blogger Needs to Know to Make Money – There is an art to writing an article that prompts the reader to make a decision to do something. That's the narrow focus of this book. You will learn how to create an article that gets a reader interested, entices them, informs them, and causes them to make a decision when they reach the end.

<u>Other Books by Richard Lowe Jr</u>

<u>How to Be Friends with Women: How to Surround Yourself with Beautiful Women without Being Sleazy</u> – I am a photographer and frequently find myself surrounded by some of the most beautiful women in the world. This book explains how men can attract women and keep them as friends, which can often lead to real, fulfilling relationships.

<u>How to Throw Parties like a Professional: Tips to Help You Succeed with Putting on a Party Event</u> – Many of us have put on parties, and I know it can be a daunting and confusing experience. In this book, I share what I learned from hosting small house parties to shows and events.

Additional Resources

Is your career important to you? Find out how to move your career in any direction you desire, improve your long-term livelihood, and be prepared for any eventuality. Visit the page below to sign up to receive valuable tips via email, and to get a free eBook about how to optimize your LinkedIn profile.

http://list.thewritingking.com/

I've written and published many books on a variety of subjects. They are all listed on the following page.

https://www.thewritingking.com/books/

On that site, I also publish articles about business, writing, and other subjects. You can visit by clicking the following link:

https://www.thewritingking.com

To find out more about me or my photography, you can visit these sites:

Personal website: https://www.richardlowe.com
Photography: http://www.richardlowejr.com
LinkedIn Profile: https://www.linkedin.com/in/richardlowejr
Twitter: https://twitter.com/richardlowejr

If you have any comments about this book, feel free to email me at rich@thewritingking.com

Additional Resources

Bonnie Dillabough, AKA The Web Woman put up her first website back in 1996 and she has been making her living online ever since.

Over the 20 plus years of her career, she has had the opportunity to work in all areas of marketing online, from website production, to video production, to SEO and social media marketing.

Her specialty is creating "netrepreneurs" as online celebrities in their specific niche. She creates custom marketing plans for small to medium-sized companies designed to help them find their tribe, to get their message in front of people who are actually looking for what they have to sell, whether that be services, products or media.

Her new digital marketing agency, Fast Forward Enterprises has a wide range of services including:

- WordPress Site Design and Installation
- Keyword Research and Strategy
- Complete Custom Marketing Strategies
- Video Marketing and Video Creation
- Walk On Video Spokespersons
- Content Creation
- Website and Business Graphic Design
- Marketing Automation
- Lead Capture Pages
- Newsletter Setup
- Article and Report Writing
- Press Release Writing and Distribution
- Ecommerce Site Setup
- Membership Site Setup
- ...and much more

To Contact The Web Woman: bonnie@akathewebwoman.com
http://fastforwardenterprises.com
910 995-3768

Premium Writing Services

Do you have a story that needs to be told? Have you been trying to write a book for ages but never can seem to find the time to get it done? Do you want to brand your business, but don't know how to get started?

The Writing King has the answer. We can help you with any of your writing needs.

Ghostwriting. We can write your book, which entails interviewing you to get your story, writing the book and then working with you to revise it until complete. To discuss your book, contact The Writing King today.

Website Copy. Many businesses include the text on their sites as an afterthought, and that can result in lost sales and leads. Hire The Writing King to review your site and recommend changes to the text which will help communicate your message and improve your sales.

Blogging. Build engagement with your customers by hiring us to write a weekly or semi-weekly article for your blog, LinkedIn or other social media. Contact The Writing King today to discuss your blogging needs.

LinkedIn. LinkedIn is of the most important vehicles for finding new business, and a professionally written profile works to pulling in those leads. Write or update your profile today.

Technical Writing. We have broad experience in the computer, warehousing and retail industries, and have

Premium Writing Services

written hundreds of technical documents. Contact The Writing King today to find out how we can help you with your technical writing project.

The Writing King has the skills and knowledge to help you with any of your writing needs. Call us today to discuss how we can help you.

www.ingramcontent.com/pod-product-compliance
Lightning Source LLC
Chambersburg PA
CBHW050454190326
41458CB00005B/1278